Michael Ondaatje's
The English Patient

CONTINUUM CONTEMPORARIES

Also available in this series:

Forthcoming in this series:

· MICHAEL ONDAATJE'S

The English Patient

A READER'S GUIDE

JOHN BOLLAND

CONTINUUM | NEW YORK | LONDON

2002

The Continuum International Publishing Group Inc
370 Lexington Avenue, New York, NY 10017

The Continuum International Publishing Group Ltd
The Tower Building, 11 York Road, London SE1 7NX

www.continuumbooks.com

Printed in the United States of America

Library of Congress Cataloging-in-Publication Data

Bolland, John, 1944-
      Michael Ondaatje's The English patient : a reader's guide / John
Bolland.
          p. cm. — (Continuum contemporaries)
      Includes bibliographical references.
      ISBN 0-8264-5243-4 (pbk. : alk. paper)
      1. Ondaatje, Michael, 1943- . English patient. 2. World War,
1939–1945 — Literature and the war. 3. Italy — In literature.
4. Egypt — In literature. I. Title: English patient. II. Title.

PR9199.3.O5 E543 2002
813'.54—dc21   2001047382

Contents

for Christine, Emily and William

Acknowledgements

Discussions with my colleagues at Manchester Metropolitan University, Daniela Caselli, Stewart Crehan, Alan Fair and John Sears, helped to focus my ideas while writing this book, and I am grateful to them.

I would like to thank Sue Smith and Mary Pickstone for their help with bibliographical searches. I would also like to thank my wife Christine for her helpful suggestions and for all the support she has given me.

1

The Novelist

In the memoir of his parents' generation, *Running in the Family*, Ondaatje wrote "I am the foreigner. I am the prodigal who hates the foreigner." The paradox points to a tension in his thought and writing: — between an identification with the figure of the outsider — whose marginality is the source of a powerful, if anarchic, creative energy and integrity of vision — and an equally felt need for belonging. As he put it in an interview in 1977, "In a way I am a very displaced person. I really envy roots." The tension between marginality and integration, severance and union is central to much of Ondaatje's work. The pattern recurs in the lives of a number of his fictional protagonists and it is also a striking feature of his own life and career to date.

Michael Ondaatje was born on 12 September, 1943, in Kegalle, about fifty miles west of Colombo, the capital of what was then Ceylon, now Sri Lanka, where his family owned a tea plantation. His father and mother came from well-established Burgher families, part of the Eurasian community who formed an important element of the Ceylonese élite. By 1945, his parents had divorced and he moved with his mother to Colombo, where he later entered St.

Thomas's College Boys' School, which even after Sri Lanka's independence was still largely modelled on British traditions. His mother moved to England, and Ondaatje joined her in 1952, after which he was never to see his father again, though they did write to one another. He went to Dulwich College, a public school with a strong academic record and long literary associations, where Ondaatje said he "became obsessed with reading." Of his time in England, Ondaatje has said, "I grew up in Sri Lanka and lived in England for about eight years, and then came [to Canada] . . . I don't feel much of 'England' in me. I *do* feel I have been allowed the migrant's double perspective, in the way, say, someone like Gertrude Stein was 're-focused' by Paris."

In 1962, at the age of nineteen, Ondaatje joined his elder brother Chris in Canada, and entered Bishop's University, an Anglican foundation, in Lennoxville, Quebec. Ondaatje was fortunate in finding inspirational teachers of literature and practising poets there and at the University of Toronto where he completed his BA Degree in 1965. George Whalley, Arthur Moyet, Doug Jones, and Ralph Gustafson encouraged his writing and made him aware of a new vigorous Canadian tradition being formed at that period, and in particular making him part of a community of poets and scholars who would gather at the Jones's summer retreat of Keeywardin. Ondaatje was to recreate the gathering of artistic friends at his own family summer retreat, The Blue Roof Farm, near Kingston.

In 1964, Ondaatje married the artist Kim Jones, and by 1967 they had two children, Quintin and Griffin. They moved to the University of Toronto and there began a phase of intense creative activity, literary and academic, and of rapid public recognition. He won the Norma Epstein award for poetry in 1965 and his poems were published in Raymond Souster's important anthology, *New Wave Canada* in 1966 (he had acquired Canadian nationality in 1965). He completed his M.A. thesis on myth in the poetry of

Edwin Muir in 1967, an interest that was to influence much of his own later work. In the same year his first collection of poems, *The Dainty Monsters*, was published by Coach House Press, and he began teaching at the University of Western Ontario. His second book, the long poem, *The Man with Seven Toes*, and a critical study of Leonard Cohen appeared in 1969, and his narrative collage, *The Collected Works of Billy the Kid: Left Handed Poems*, for which he received the Governor General's award, in 1970.

In 1971, Ondaatje's teaching contract at Western Ontario was not renewed. He had been unwilling to complete the Ph.D. required by the English Department, and in an atmosphere of bitterness and controversy (caused in part by student support for him as a popular teacher) he left the University. In the same year, however, he was appointed to a teaching post at Glendon College, York University, where he "began teaching poetry from the perspective of a practising writer" (Jewinski, p. 85), and his own creative output was resumed: his next poetry collection, *Rat Jelly*, appeared in 1973; his fictionalized biography of the jazz cornet player, Buddy Bolden, *Coming Through Slaughter* (1976), was co-winner of the Books in Canada First Novel Award. The humorous chapbook, *Elimination Dance* (1978), was followed by the poetry collection, *There's A Trick With A Knife I'm Learning to Do* (1979), for which he received the Governor General's Award.

In 1978, Ondaatje returned to Ceylon, now Sri Lanka, and spent five months of sabbatical leave collecting material for his semi-fictional memoir, *Running in the Family*, which was published in 1982. It was at this time that his marriage came under strain. He spent 1981 as Visiting Professor at the University of Hawaii. While there he met the television journalist and producer, Linda Spalding, and in the following year separated from his wife. As Ed Jewinski suggests, the poems he wrote about this period in *Tin Roof* (1982) and *Secular Love* (1984) are a painful record of separation and loss, and this was also the time in which Ondaatje's "wrestling . . . with [the] sense of where he belonged was becoming more and more urgent" (Jewinski, p. 112).

If *Running in the Family* was written in response to the need to explore the source of his own identity, it was also the work in which there first emerged the political themes that were to occupy Ondaatje in his next three novels, the relation of the politically and economically marginalized to the dominant structures of power. *In the Skin of A Lion* was published in 1987, and established his reputation nationally and internationally, receiving the Order of Canada in addition to numerous other awards; a selection of his poems, *The Cinammon Peeler*, was published in Great Britain in 1989; *The English Patient* was published in 1992 and won the Booker Prize, the Governor General's Award and the Trillium Award. His latest works, the collection of poems, *Handwriting* (1998), and the novel, *Anil's Ghost* (2000), show a revival of interest in the landscape, culture and politics of Sri Lanka.

Ondaatje's creative interests have ranged across a number of fields. He has had a substantial achievement as an editor, of journals and collections of poetry and fiction, and has been generous in his support for the work of other young Canadian writers. He has also shown an active interest in art, photography, drama and film. A number of his earlier works have been staged and he has directed two films. The first, *Sons of Captain Poetry* (1965), was a short film on the Canadian poet, bp Nichol, during which Nichol discusses the influence of the Dadaists. Jewinski suggests that the Dadaists' creative exploitation of "chance and accident, of random, illogical juxtapositions" (Jewinski, p. 72), determined the content and structure of the film, and a fondness for contingency and unpredictability has certainly been a significant formal feature of all Ondaatje's own work. His next film, *The Clinton Special* (1972), was another documentary, in a freestyle, on a farming community in Ontario. For

Ondaatje, filmmaking and writing were mutually influential crea-tive activities. He was an avid student of the techniques used in films like Sergio Leone's *Once Upon a Time in the West*, and Leone's alternation of static photographic effects with rapid action, has influenced the pacing of Ondaatje's narratives, which also show a familiarity with the whole vocabulary of cinema — cutting from scene to scene, montage, tracking.

THE CANADIAN CULTURAL CONTEXT

Ondaatje's interest in the figure of the outsider was influenced by his own experience of migration and later by his concern to under-stand the particular form of cultural hybridity experienced by his family in Ceylon. However, in the 1990 interview with Linda Hutcheon, Ondaatje agreed to her definition of him as a Sri Lankan *Canadian* writer, and to Catherine Bush he cited as amongst his earliest influences Canadian writers such as A. M. Klein, Phyllis Webb, Raymond Souster, David McFadden and bp Nichol. It is significant that the 1960s, when Ondaatje was at a formative stage as a writer in Canada, were a period in which concepts of national identity were being questioned and re-defined through an increas-ing recognition of the importance of marginalized social groups.

As a bilingual country, colonized by the British and French, with distinct cultural traditions and allegiances, Canada's national iden-tity has always been a sensitive cultural and political issue. Earlier historians like Arthur Lowe had defined this identity as a continua-tion of British and French political structures and cultures into the environment and climate of Canada. The characteristic mode of frontier life was the family farmstead in which a harsh climate and frequently infertile soil had been the source of a distinctive experi-ence and psychology. The "frontier psychology," a purifying encounter between individual and a vast, hostile landscape, a lifestyle based on "the puritannical restraint which masks the psychological tension set up by the contrast of wilderness and home discipline" (Mandel, pp. 52–53), continues to be a reference point in a number of Ondaatje's poems and narratives. It is significant that *The English Patient* ends with Hana's letter to her stepmother, *"I am sick of Europe, Clara. I want to come home. To your small cabin and pink rock in Georgian Bay. I will take a bus up to Parry Sound. And from the mainland send a message over the shortwave radio out towards the Pancakes. And wait for you, wait to see the silhouette of you in a canoe coming to rescue me from this place we all entered, betraying you"* (p. 296, italics in original).

As Carl Berger shows, the 1960s mark a turning-point in Canadian historiography. In contrast to earlier periods dominated by a small homogeneous group of men of British descent, the expansion of education in the 1960s brought people of a more varied cultural, ethnic and gender background into the field. They often brought a determination to revise the existing history from the perspective of hitherto subordinate groups. The "New History" sought to uncover the lives of those who had been denied a role in Canada's past: women, immigrants, the working class. History was also now seen to have been dominated by the perspective of the colonizer. The debate about Canadian history understandably made a strong impact on Ondaatje. In an interview with Catherine Bush in 1990, he said

I think reclaiming untold stories is an essential role for the writer. Especially in this country, where one can no longer trust the media. The newspapers have such power over the story and portrait of Canada. You can see the newspapers moving in a certain politically right-wing or economically right-wing direction, and this—before you know it—becomes the official voice of the country . . . (Bush, p. 147)

The emergence of Post-Colonial literature and theory as an increasingly important field in literary studies in the 1970s and 1980s gave a further impetus to the re-assessment of Canadian national identity, particularly in its relation to the European colonial powers and to the native people of Canada. The term "post-colonial" has been used to describe ways of theorizing or representing subjective experience and forms of resistance within cultures that have undergone or been affected by colonialism. As a "Second World," settler colony, Canada's experience of and resistance to colonialism has been complex and ambivalent. According to Mark Lawson, the settler subject is characterized by a divided sense of identity: "Settler post-imperial cultures are divided between 'mother and other', simultaneously colonized and colonizing" (Lawson, p. 25). Stephen Slemon suggests that "the *illusion* of a stable self/other, here/there binary divide has *never* been available to Second World [settler] writers," and resistance has therefore been marked by ambivalence in settler post-colonial writing, which has employed strategies to express a sense of opposition to *and* complicity with the colonial power (Slemon, p. 38).

Ondaatje's early work was published by small presses in Canada, Coach House and Anansi, which promoted the work of a group of writers who have come to be associated with a distinctively Canadian post-modern aesthetic. In her study, *The Canadian Postmodern* (1988), Linda Hutcheon has included Ondaatje in this movement together with Leonard Cohen, Robert Kroetsch, Margaret Atwood, and Alice Munro, and linked it to the new forms of political and national consciousness that emerged in the 1960s as Canadians began to question hitherto dominant British and French traditions and increasingly to recognize marginal groups as the site of a particularly dynamic and significant voice.

It is beyond the scope of the present study to provide a comprehensive account of post-modernism, but it will be useful to examine the term as a descriptor of aspects of late twentieth social consciousness which have a particular bearing on the Canadian experience and the work of Ondaatje. François Lyotard's classic work, *The Postmodern Condition: A Report on Knowledge* (originally published in French, 1979), defined the postmodern as "incredulity toward metanarratives" (p. xxiv). Lyotard argues that in the past there had been a consensus about the purpose and direction of society, based on certain themes, such as the universal belief in the right of every individual to freedom through education and knowledge, or the Marxist belief in the emancipation of the people from class domination. Postmodernism describes a condition in which there has been a widespread loss of faith in such sustaining narratives, and a crisis about the basis of legitimation in any field of knowledge. In historiography, for example, as Hutcheon suggests, "[no] longer is history to be accepted as 'how things actually happened' . . . [but] as a construction, as having been *made* by the historian through a process of selecting, ordering and narrating" (*CP*, pp. 14–15). In place of the authoritative truths of the past, postmodern knowledge is characterized by "a sensitivity to differences" (Lyotard), a recognition of the heterogeneity of systems through which knowledge is validated.

From its initial concern with history, postmodernism has extended its concern with the foundations of knowledge to the way in which reality is represented in specific cultures. Postmodernism in the arts has been concerned to show how our experience of the world is not spontaneous but the product of conventions governing perception. Postmodernist works are thus characterized by 'self-reflexivity,' by strategies that foreground the formal conventions through which reality is artistically represented. According to Hutcheon, postmodernism's celebration of difference was particularly suited to the Canadian cultural context of the 1960s when uniform concepts of national identity were being challenged by the recognition of cultural difference. Furthermore, she suggests,

Canadian postmodern novels offer yet another example of the self-conscious or "meta"-sensibility, that is, the awareness that all our systems of understanding are deliberate and historically specific constructs (not natural and eternal givens). (*CP*, p. x)

Always subversive of the culture of which he or she is a part, the postmodern writer is "in an ex-centric position with regard to the dominant culture," and "since the periphery or the margin might also describe Canada's perceived position in international terms, perhaps the postmodern ex-centric is very much a part of the identity of the nation" (*CP*, p. 3).

FORMAL AND THEMATIC DEVELOPMENT TO *THE ENGLISH PATIENT*

Ondaatje first made his literary reputation through his poetry, which reflects many of the thematic and aesthetic concerns of his later fictional works. His earliest critics, George Bowering, Sam Solecki and Douglas Barbour, recognized that, as Solecki put it, "a tension between mind and chaos is at the centre of Ondaatje's poetry." In *The Dainty Monsters* (1967), this tension is expressed through a confrontation between the violent otherness of animals and a more benign domestic reality. Increasingly, in "Peter," or the drunken narrator of "Claude Glass," or the figure of his father in "Letters and Other Worlds," Ondaatje finds human exemplars of a dimension of experience outside the social. Locked in an isolated private world of pain, violence to self and others, these figures are heroic by virtue of "sailing to that perfect edge/ where there is no social fuel/ Release of sandbags/ to understand their altitude" ("White Dwarfs," *Rat Jelly*, p. 70). As a poet, Ondaatje's task is to harness such intensity to artistic form without sacrificing the anarchic energy which is the source of creative power: "My mind is pouring chaos/ in nets onto the page" ("The Gate in His Head," *Rat Jelly*, p. 62).

Ondaatje's poetry shows an increasing recognition of the value of community, which is reflected in his later fictional work. In "The Diverse Causes," the narrator finds "a civilized magic," a decorum and grace, in the interactions of family life and routines of domesticity, while in "The Concessions" and "Red Accordion — an immigrant song," Ondaatje is the migrant poet celebrating new bonds of affiliation,

> *All of us poised and inspired by music*
> *friendship self-made heat and the knowledge*
> *each has chosen to come here driven for hours*
> *over iced highways, to be here bouncing and leaping*
>
> *to a reel that carried itself generations ago*
> *north of the border, through lost towns,*
> *settled among the strange names,*
> *and became eventually our own*
>
> *all the way from Virginia.*
>> ("Red Accordion: an immigrant song,"
>> *The Cinammon Peeler*, p. 184)

Such poems find in the immediacy of physical sensation a source of value that is set against the historical past, a contrast that recurs in Ondaatje's later fiction, including *The English Patient*. In "Walking to Bellrock," "[the] plot of the afternoon is to get to Bellrock/ through rapids, falls, stink water . . ." (*CP*, p. 63), and this overrides in its vivid urgency the remoter narratives of logging history that the poem alludes to. In "Pig Glass" and "The Palace," as in *The English Patient*, there is a sense of the present superimposed on layers of history which the modern-day narrator is trying to excavate.

Ondaatje's MA thesis was on the role of myth in the poetry of Edwin Muir, and he has expressed his admiration for "the raw power of myth" in Howard O'Hagan's novel, *Tay John*. His poem, "In Another Fashion," anounces a poetic manifesto in which

> We must build new myths
> to wind up the world,
> provoke new christs
> with our beautiful women,
> bring
>
> plumed
> thin boned birds
> to claw carpets
> to betray
> majesty in a sway
>
> Pale birds
> with rings on ugly feet
> to drink from clear bowls
> to mate with our children.
>   (*The Dainty Monsters*,
>   p. 34)

Myth's function is "to wind up the world," to raise experience to the intensity of art. This is done partly by recurrence, either by linking subject matter to narratives or vocabulary from the past—as in this poem the domestic is transmuted through the reference to Leda and the swan—or, as Ondaatje suggests, by establishing new patterns by "repeating and building images and so making them

more potent . . . Myth is achieved by a very careful use of echoes—
of phrases and images." It is also the violence of his images that
gains Ondaatje's poetry "the raw power of myth"—for example, the
juxtapositioning of delicacy and destructive power in "Heron Rex,"
the narrator's description of "headless Tom" in "Elizabeth," the
disembowelling of Paris in "Troy Town," or the precise description
of the dying agony of the construction worker in "For Tom Falling."

Ondaatje explores the relation between violence and creativity
most fully in *The Collected Works of Billy the Kid: Left-Handed
Poems* (1970). Described as "a narrative collage," it consists of generic fragments—interviews, newspaper articles, photographs, historical extracts, passages of lyric poetry, comic strip, surrealism and
objective factual description. *The Collected Works'* rejection of formal boundaries is paralleled by its choice of hero as outsider, often
literally placed on boundaries—between Canada and the United
States, in a doorway between bright sun and "cold dark," smashing
an arm through a window pane; its title views the outlaw's cycle of
killing as a literary oeuvre, and the spectacle of bloodshed working
upon an imagination like Billy's often effects a poetic estrangement
from routine habits of perception: ". . . one turns when the bullet
leaves you/ walk off see none of the thrashing/ the very eyes welling
up like bad drains" (p. 11). As Stephen Scobie suggests, Ondaatje's
Billy is in the tradition of the Romantic artist, whose position as
outsider gives a level of perception above the utilitarian norm; he
also exemplifies Ondaatje's conception of art as holding a precarious
balance between violent energy and formal beauty—like "great
stars" "straining to the centre/ that would explode their white/ if
temperature and the speed they moved at/ shifted one degree"
(p. 41). Ondaatje's artist-outsiders are haunted by "the one altered
move" that will make their creative power "maniac." Billy's antith-
esis is the sherrif Pat Garrett, who captures and finally kills him,
and who represents a discipline and control that preys upon spon-

taneous, creative energy. The central opposition between Billy and Garrett is replicated in a series of contrasts: violent energy is figured in the awesome power of the sun, the orgiastic sex between Billy and Angie Dickinson, and scenes depicting animals or humans in a frenzy of killing, while order finds a positive image in the haven of companionship, peace and shade found in the Chisum ranch and particularly focused on Sallie Chisum.

The crossing of genre borders is matched by the disruption of narrative form in *The Collected Works* in a way that looks forward to the narrative techniques of *The English Patient*. From the opening where Billy describes his own death in the past, linear narrative is subverted, and the story proceeds through flashback, anticipation and repetitions. As Douglas Barbour suggests, the fragments that constitute Billy's life "refuse to assume an overarching narrative shape," and the use of shifting narrative viewpoints — Pat Garrett, Sallie Chisum, Paulita Maxwell, the newspaper reporter, comic book — present a hero whose identity defies definition: "Not a story about me through their eyes then. Find the beginning, the slight silver key to unlock it, to dig it out. Here then is a maze to begin, be in" (*CWBK*, p. 20). The conflict between creative and destructive energy is returned to in Ondaatje's first novel, *Coming Through Slaughter* (1976), in the figure of the New Orleans jazz cornet player, Buddy Bolden. There is a persistent connection between Bolden's creative drive and violence, figured in the act in which he lashes out at a window, holding back at the last moment so that the "window starred and crumpled slowly two floors down" (p. 16), but the balance between violence and creative energy is too precarious, and after a climactic performance in a New Orleans parade, he lapses into madness and silence. Ondaatje's artist heroes seek "a loss of privacy" (*CTS*, p. 130), a transcendence of self through the intensity of their art, the violence of their lives, or the intensity of sexual passion. The scenes between Bolden and Robin Brewitt look forward to those between Katharine and Almásy in *The English Patient*. Sex is an escape from the habitual into an alien self. It is a "step past the territory" (*CTS*, p. 62), past limits of identity through a merging with the other, "a slow true intimacy" that involves "a disintegration [of the lovers] after they exchanged personalities and mannerisms" (p. 88).

Up to 1978, Ondaatje's concern with the outsider had focused on the individual, in particular the figure of the artist. There is a relative lack of interest in the issue of race in his portrait of Buddy Bolden, and in 1983 he was criticized by Arun Mukherjee for "the absence of any cultural baggage he might have brought with him [from Sri Lanka]," and for "siding with the colonizer." In 1978 and 1980, however, he made two visits to Sri Lanka to research the material for his family memoir, *Running in the Family* (1982). The island's history of invasion, colonization, and ethnic intermixing made it inevitable for Ondaatje to consider the issue of identity in relation to social, political and economic structures, and this has become a feature of all his subsequent writing.

Sri Lanka has a long tradition of ethnic, religious and cultural diversity, with significant Catholic, Protestant and Islamic minorities co-existing with the two main religions, Buddhist and Hindu. Independence was granted in 1948, since when tension developed between the two main ethnic groups, the majority Sinhalese, mainly Buddhist, and the Tamils, mainly Hindu. It culminated in a protracted and bloody civil war over the Tamil demand for an independent state.

Sri Lankan politics has been dominated by an élite consisting largely of Sinhalese and Tamils, in addition to the British administrators of the colonial period. The Eurasians were the miscegenous offspring of European colonizers, and this group had considerable economic power through ownership of land. It was part of the élite by virtue of its European blood, and it was to this group that

Ondaatje's family belonged. Ondaatje's researches into his family's past represent a decisive stage in his approach to issues of identity. The contradictions of the Eurasian community—its assimilation and rejection of British traditions and role models, its detachment from Sinhalese and Tamil communities and political projects— gave a more precise sociological dimension to his interest in the displaced, outsider figure. Throughout the 1920s, the Eurasian élite enjoyed a wild, roistering lifestyle, whose "vivid" unconventionality appealed to Ondaatje's love for those who live on the social edge. With independence, some of the Eurasians, in particular Ondaatje's family, became increasingly marginalized socially and economically, a process that he records with sympathy.

The Eurasian community represented in *Running in the Family* celebrated its hybridity—"Everyone was vaguely related and had Sinhalese, Tamil, Dutch, British and Burgher blood in them going back many generations" (p. 41). This gave them an irreverent aloofness to the political aspirations of the two main Asian ethnic groups and to the British Imperialists ("seen as transients, racists, and snobs"), while it also seems to have encouraged a blindness to the disparity between the wealth of the élite and the masses. As first person narrator, Ondaatje's attitude to the British and the tradition of Empire is attended with complexities. His parents and grandather were steeped in British values, and yet British cultural models— dances, theatricals, novels, games of croquet—were interpreted with such brilliant excess that the effect is one of parody. In *Running in the Family*, parody becomes a way of negotiating a complex relation to the dominant tradition—to express a sense of living in that tradition while subverting its authority through playful excess, and this is a strategy that will be encountered again in *The English Patient*.

Running in the Family continues Ondaatje's interest in characters whose creativity stems from living on the edge, where exuberant non-conformity — "They were all laughing, crazy, and vivid in their prime" — often entailed the "waste of youth. Burned purposeless." This was most obviously exemplified in the father, Mervyn Ondaatje, whose alternating bouts of charming eccentricity and alcoholic violence culminated in withdrawal, silence and depression like that of Bolden.

In the poetic memoir to his family, "Light," Ondaatje writes "These are their fragments, all I remember, /wanting more knowledge" (*Cinammon Peeler*, p. 5), and the lines point to a structural feature of much of his work — the narrative quest for a character whose identity eludes, the father whom he felt he never understood, who must be constructed from fragments of different witnesses that resist finality and closure. The sense of ontological instability is linked in *Running in the Family* to postmodern strategies which undermine claims to absolute knowledge and truth. The empirical emphasis on exact dates and locations is juxtaposed with gossipy anecdote — "No story is ever told just once. Whether a memory or funny hideous scandal, we will return to it an hour later and retell the story with additions and this time with a few judgements thrown in. In this way history is organized" (p. 26) — and this anticipates the role of Herodotus in *The English Patient* in its playful subversion of hierarchies of fact and fiction.

In the Skin of A Lion (1987), the first of Ondaatje's works to approximate to a conventional novel, is also the first to engage explicitly with a political theme. The novel deals with the role of immigrant workers excluded from the official history of the building of Toronto. The political theme thus coincides with the postmodernist challenge to dominant narratives and in particular with Ondaatje's concern to reclaim untold stories. Ondaatje spent time at the city archives and with the resources of the Multicultural History Society of Ontario, to establish the historical context of Canada and in particular Toronto in the 1920s and 1930s. Notable events and figures in the written record, like the Commissioner of Public Works, Harris, and the building of the Bloor Street Viaduct, are described but juxtaposed with the untold stories, the oral narratives of the Macedonian and Italian workers, "who actually built the goddamned bridge".

As has been seen, in settler colonies like Canada, protest against dominant political and economic structures is often complicated by a sense of complicity with the exploiting élite. In Ondaatje's case, the experience of Canadian cultural politics is overlaid by his own sense of being a migrant and by the recognition of his family's contradictory relation to British imperial power and culture in Sri Lanka. It is significant, therefore, that he chooses as his central protagonist a figure who experiences a conflicted sense of identity and loyalty. Patrick Lewis's family had been homesteaders since the Nineteenth Century, and their lifestyle typified the ascetic, puritannical industriousness seen as defining national identity by the early Canadian historians (Patrick Lewis is Hana's stepfather who dies of his burns in *The English Patient*). Despite being part of the dominant race and tradition, Patrick feels himself to be an alien — like Ondaatje he sees himself as both foreigner and son of the land. When he finds work as a construction worker on the viaduct, Patrick becomes aware of the immigrant workers' communities which he had previously regarded as a mysterious other. He finds new forms of solidarity, based not on genealogical descent but collaboration in labor and in forms of social and cultural expression. He befriends the Italian-Canadian thief, Caravaggio, when the latter is a victim of a racial attack, and he becomes a political revolutionary. However, Patrick's political commitment is uncertain. As in *The English Patient*, personal relationships are shown to be more potent forms of resisting capitalist economic interests: "I don't believe the language of politics, but I'll protect the friends I have" (p. 122).

2

The Novel

INTRODUCTION

"**K**ip and I are international bastards," the English patient announces, and in an interview Ondaatje has said of *The English Patient* (1992), "There are a lot of international bastards roaming around the world today. That's one of the book's main stories. Those migrants don't belong here but want to belong here and find a new home" (Wachtel, p. 260). Clearly, displacement and exile are core experiences which the novel seeks to explore. The group that gathers at the Villa San Girolamo at the end of World War II are all exiles from their homeland.

We are first introduced to Hana—a Canadian nurse of mixed parentage as we learn from Ondaatje's earlier novel *In the Skin of A Lion*—who has volunteered for war service and is posted to Italy. The father of her unborn child has been killed. Continuously surrounded by the dying, she feels desensitized to human suffering and the news of her father's death by burns brings her close to nervous collapse. Unable to face the prospect of bringing a child into such a world, she has an abortion. When the rest of the Canadian Infantry Division continues the advance up Italy, she stays behind to nurse the dying burnt figure who has come to be called the English patient. It is partly a consecration of herself to the memory of her father, but also a means of achieving some form of salvation, for herself, and in a deeper sense, perhaps, for a cursed land.

In the patient himself and Kirpal Singh, the Sikh who becomes a sapper in the British army, the novel offers us characters who represent a cultural hybridity which rejects national borders — even though the ending sees the affirmation of a Sikh identity and the assertion of a nationalist politics. Kirpal Singh shows an alienation from his birth family, familiar in Ondaatje's work. He rejects his family traditions and in contrast with his more anti-colonial brother, joins the British army in England. Despite some initial feelings of exclusion, he finds a new family in the bomb disposal squad commanded by Lord Suffolk, who becomes a surrogate father. Rechristened Kip, he becomes a lover of things English. His expertise, technological knowledge, sense of discipline and order, and courage in defusing bombs, gain him respect and establish in him a confident sense of identity in his adopted land. The deaths of Lord Suffolk and his assistant, Miss Morden, however, remove points of reference that had provided a temporary stability and leaving the bomb disposal unit, Kip joins the sappers in the Italian Campaign. Here he discovers Hana caring for her patient in a dangerously unstable villa abandoned by the advancing Allied forces. They are linked by a shared experience of grieving for lost fathers. At first self-sufficient and introverted, Kip begins to re-establish bonds of relationship again through affection for the patient and his love for Hana. He feels integrated into a community once more and celebrates this by organizing a birthday dinner for Hana. But the sense of community proves temporary. News of the atomic bombs on Hiroshima and Nagasaki confirms for him the fundamental barriers between East and West, between the white and brown races, and abandoning the group at the villa he rides off on his motorbike, seemingly on a new quest. The novel's epilogue shows him having re-established his identity as the Sikh, Kirpal Singh, and, according to his family's tradition for the second son, he becomes a doctor serving the local community in a Punjabi village.

The story of the English patient himself is reconstructed in the novel from jottings in diaries, fragments of memories often under the influence of morphine, and from additional evidence provided by his interrogator Caravaggio. An element of uncertainty is created about some of the main facts of his life. As Count Ladislaus de Almásy, he had joined a group of German, English, Hungarian, and African explorers in the early 1930s searching for the lost oasis of Zerzura. They were an "oasis society," and "gradually [they] became nationless" (p. 138, references to the Picador edition), though, as World War II approached, Almásy notes that they began to betray personal loyalties for the sake of nationalistic rivalry. Joined by the Cliftons, aristocratic English newlyweds, there is initially animosity between Katharine Clifton and Almásy, but this soon develops into an intense adulterous passion. Their affair is set in Cairo and threatens the social boundaries and controls of expatriate Cairo society. Katharine's husband, who unknown to the group has been tracking their explorations for British Intelligence, discovers his wife's infidelity, which makes for a subtle contrast between different forms of betrayal. In 1939, Clifton flies with Katharine to the base camp where Almásy is collecting equipment, and tries to kill them all with his plane. Clifton dies, but though she is seriously injured, Katharine and Almásy survive the crash, and he leaves her in the Cave of Swimmers to make the long desert trek for transport. When Almásy meets a stray English outfit, he fails to give Katharine's married name, the proof of her British identity, and, taken for a spy, he is refused assistance. Desperate to return to her, Almásy turns to the Germans, who agree to provide transport in exchange for his help in guiding the spy Eppler across the desert to Cairo. After a period in which he appears to have collaborated with Rommel, he does return in 1942 to the Cave of Swimmers. He paints Katharine's dead body with pigments from the prehistoric cave paintings, and carries it to a plane that had been left many years before near the base camp. Though he succeeds in taking off, inevitably the plane catches fire. Almásy breaks the glass of the cockpit, parachutes to the earth, his body aflame, in the striking image that opens the novel. He is saved by a group of nomads for whom the concept of nations is meaningless.

The fourth member of the villa is the Italian-Canadian, Caravaggio, another character carried over from *In the Skin of A Lion*, where he was a friend of Hana's father and in this novel is shown to have developed a deep affection for the child Hana. Recognizing his brilliance as a thief, the Allies recruit him as a spy working for British intelligence in Cairo. After some dashing escapades after the German capture of Cairo, he is finally arrested and threatened with the amputation of his fingers unless he reveals secret information. He resists, until the amputation of his thumbs forces him to reveal identities. Like the English patient, obsessed with the failure of his relationship with Katharine and his failure to save her life, Caravaggio is haunted by memories of his torture. Though the novel is not explicit about his motives, a combination of personal guilt at betrayal, desire to exact revenge and to set Hana free from her obsession with the patient, makes him seek out Almásy, determined to establish his identity as the spy who helped Rommel. As, under interrogation, the complexities of the patient/Almásy's motives and situation are finally revealed, questions of national betrayal come to seem irrelevant in comparison with the personal bonds Caravaggio has established with the patient.

In their different ways, all the individuals in the villa have endured physical and psychological wounds, and as Ondaatje suggests,

"It is a book about very tentative healing among a group of people. I think it is that most of all," and the villa "was an Eden, an escape, a cul-de-sac during the war and this was where the healing began" (Wachtel pp. 256, 252). Nationalism is implicated in their suffering in a number of ways: they are all victims of the violence of a war pursued for nationalistic ends; their complex heritage causes problems of identification and allegiance; their stories are linked by the theme of betrayal, which exemplifies the conflict between personal commitment to individual or group and the more abstract allegiance to nationhood and state. As will be seen in the rest of this study, the issue of identity and nationalism is explored in *The English Patient* through a number of related themes, the body, sexual relationship, and mapping, and it is formally and thematically developed through the nexus of ideas and textual practices associated with "postmodernism": the problematizing of history, intertextuality, the crossing of generic boundaries and disruption of conventional narrative form. In *The English Patient*, these themes and formal practices work to undermine the concept of a homogeneous cultural identity on which nationalism is founded: "Erase nations!"

THE EX-CENTRIC SUBJECT

Cultural theory has recognized that identity does not emerge from a spontaneous essential selfhood, but that it is largely determined by the relationship between self and other. You identify yourself as the member of an ethnic group or nation through your difference from a perceived "foreigner," as member of a class through difference from an "outsider." Such clarity of definition, however, is absent from Ondaatje's autobiographical comment, "I am the foreigner. I am the prodigal who hates the foreigner," which merges the categories of native and alien, self and other. It is absent also from his semi-fictional account of the Eurasian community to which his family belonged in Ceylon. In the description of his family circle in *Running in the Family*, self and other, oppressor and oppressed, rather than being clearly differentiated, overlap in complex ways — British with Tamil, racist with victim of racism, metropolitan culture with peripheral, class insider with class outsider. Furthermore, his personal experience of migration, first to England and then to Canada, developed a complex sense of self in Ondaatje, as he has recognized — "I *do* feel I have been granted the migrant's double perspective. . . ." Significantly, he arrived in Canada at a time when traditional concepts of national identity were being destabilized through an increasing recognition of the role of previously marginalized groups — the indigenous population of Indians and Inuits, and the waves of immigrants who were not of Anglo-French stock.

Ondaatje's rejection of the simple opposition of native and foreigner, self and other, his adoption of "the migrant's double perspective," corresponds with the way that the politics of identity have been refocused in recent post-colonial theory. The work of Homi Bhabha has attached particular significance to the position of the exile and migrant. Situated on the boundary between foreign and native, the migrant's is a strategically important location that disturbs the simple binary oppositions on which racist and colonial discourse depends. The Canadian critics Linda Hutcheon and Ajay Heble have used the term "ex-centric subject" to describe the concept of subjectivity found in writers like Ondaatje, who position themselves outside the oppressive structures of native/alien, self/other from which nationalist languages derive their meaning and "center."

The concept of the ex-centric subject is figured in the characters of the English patient and Kip. The novel's central figure is the patient himself, "A man with no face. An ebony pool. All identification consumed in a fire" (p. 48). His physical appearance images the erasure of national identity. His collaboration in the Western project to delineate, name and so possess the unmapped desert has resulted in the obliteration of his own features, the map of his identity.

Neither Kip nor the patient represents a unified, homogeneous self. The patient's identity as English is exposed by Caravaggio's later identification of him as the Hungarian Almásy and even this identification, it is hinted, might not have been conclusive — "Maybe he's Sansom" (p. 165). "*Who is he speaking as now?* Caravaggio thinks" (p. 244). From the first, his identity has been uncertain, with different allegiances and traditions overlaying him in a way that even he finds confusing:

During this time with these [Bedouin] people, he could not remember where he was from. He could have been, for all he knew, the enemy he had been fighting from the air. (p. 6)

Where was he? What civilisation was this that understood the predictions of weather and light? El Ahmar or El Abyadd, for they must be one of the northwest desert tribes . . . His favourite garden in the world had been the grass garden at Kew, the colours so delicate and various, like levels of ash on a hill. (pp. 8–9)

The patient's very Englishness is a matter of quoting familiar stereotypes, Kew Gardens, trout streams, "flower beds in Gloucestershire," birdcalls, "ask me about Don Bradman. Ask me about marmite," suggesting that it is a cultural identity that is mimicked, in the same way that "his voice . . . bring[s] forth a flutter of the English woodthrush he said was found only in Essex" (p. 112). Mimicry and parody are characteristic of post-colonial literature. These rhetorical strategies allow the text to inhabit the dominant culture while maintaining an ironic distance from it.

Uncomfortable in the social role demanded by Cairo society, the English patient seems most himself in the territorial margins of the desert, "slipping between the enemy," or in the liminal zone between signifier and referent, at the point where the world is becoming language: "It was as if he had walked under the milli-metre of haze just above the inked fibres of a map, that pure zone between land and chart between distances and legend between nature and storyteller ... The place they had come to, to be their best selves, to be unconscious of ancestry" (p. 146). The account of his intercourse with Katharine's corpse near the end of the novel is the violation of another boundary, between the living and dead.

Kip, the sapper who comes upon the group in the villa, is also a character who represents the in-between identity of the migrant. On joining the bomb disposal squad, "He stepped into a family, after a year abroad as if he were the prodigal returned" (p. 189), in a way that carries an autobiographical echo: "There was something in me that was able to click into having to become an Englishman" (Wachtel, p. 159). He is "a man from Asia who has in these last years of war assumed English fathers, following their codes like a dutiful son" (p. 217). He is assimilated into English culture and discourse, re-named Kip (an abbreviation of Kipling, and a near homophone for Kipling's *Kim*), surrounded by landmarks of British geography and tradition — the White Horse, Lord Suffolk, a subor-dinate, Hardy, to whom, inevitably, he says "Kiss me" after defusing a bomb. And yet Kip's incorporation is not simply a submission to the dominant culture. The spectacle of the young Sikh defusing a bomb in the Old Kent Road, singing *"They're changing guard at Buckingham Palace/ Christopher Robin went down with Alice"* (p. 211), suggests that the alien has assumed the totemic role of defend-ing the monarch and the irony destabilizes the image of a homoge-neous "British" identity.

The anonymity of the patient's blackened exterior becomes an emptiness which the others try to fill through projections of their own needs. Hana sees him as every man who has died, as her father who was also burned. Kip initially finds in him an image of the paternal relation between England and India which had been represented in Lord Suffolk, and later, after the bombing of Hiroshima and Nagasaki, he comes to stand for a British Imperialism finally revealed in its callous indifference to Asia. The English patient is an "ebony pool" for Hana, and the metaphor invites an exploratory descent into deeper and deeper levels of the past to find an identity that eludes — "The Englishman left long ago, Hana, he's with the Bedouin or in some English garden with its phlox and shit." (p. 122) — finally to be incarnated as Wepwawet "the jackal in the cave who will guide and protect [Katharine]" (p. 258).

The novel is at one level a war-time spy story and the context of espionage reinforces its concern with the unstable shifting self. As Catherine Bush suggests to Ondaatje in an interview, his narratives are often structured around the search for a missing person, and he agrees that "there's a physical parallel [with] the writer trying to get a fix on someone or trying to understand or hold someone long enough to understand him . . ." (Bush, pp. 241–2). The main thrust of the espionage plot is to expose the English patient as the spy Almásy, but the identification never quite becomes conclusive, so that Caravaggio's relentless interrogations come to symbolize an identity that resists final definition. The espionage plot is reversed when it emerges that all along Clifton has been spying on the Zerzura expedition, so that even the quintessentially "solid" English aristocrat provides only an illusion of identity, a synthetic, constructed self.

Ondaatje has always been aware of the relation between power and knowledge, where the desire to name and so fix identities has been an essential strategy for incorporating subjects into the orbit of colonial power. There was, therefore, a particular aptness in placing the patient in war-time Egypt and North Africa, riven by espionage and counter-espionage, where it was, ironically, the agents of imperial power who embarked on an elaborate game of fabulation: "Working in Cairo during the early days of the war, [Caravaggio] had been trained to invent double agents or phantoms who would take on flesh. He had been in charge of a mythical agent named 'Cheese', and he spent weeks clothing him with facts, giving him qualities of character . . ." (p. 117). The proliferation of names, Cheese, Cicero, Delilah, Rebecca produces an excess of signification within the Imperial war machine itself, slipping the link between language and reality, undermining the determinate identities through which the dominant power draws subjects into its sphere of knowledge.

The inhabitants of the Villa are all displaced individuals who begin "shedding [the] skins" of earlier selves, and find new identities through the relationships they form in their Tuscan refuge. Two scenes in particular, dancing to the music of the Gershwins and Lorenz Hart and the birthday dinner for Hana, celebrate the forging of a new community which crosses barriers of age, culture and gender and which is cut off from the violence of the outside world controlled by money and power: "Just fifty yards away, there had been no representation of them in the world . . ." (p. 112). In these scenes, *The English Patient* shows a pattern of development which Ajay Heble identified in *In the Skin of A Lion*, in which relationships based on affiliation come to replace those based on birth and place of origin. "Filiation" and "affiliation" are Edward Said's terms for two distinct forms of belonging that are critical in our understanding of contemporary consciousness. Filiation describes relationships based on some form of "direct genealogical descent," for natural and biological continuity between generations, whereas "affiliation" is his term for relationships based on "social and political conviction, economic and historical circumstances, voluntary effort and willed deliberation" (Heble, p. 242, quoting Said). Kip's biological family had failed to provide him with security, and he finds a series of surrogate fathers in the novel, his commanding officer, Lord Suffolk, the figure of Isaiah in the bible, and the English patient. Like Hana, another character cut off from her biological family, Kip finds a new family in the villa, one based on affiliation, the voluntary formation of a community by individuals of different nationalities.

The group in the villa represents a postnational conception of identity—"We are all international bastards." However, increasingly Kip begins to assert a nationalist politics and an ethnic identity based on a filiative tradition going back to ancient times (see, for example, p. 271). Earlier he had resisted his brother's advocacy of an Asian solidarity against the West by pointing to Japanese brutality to Sikhs, but the nuclear bombing of Hiroshima and Nagasaki convinces him that the binary structures of Europe and Asia, black and white—which the novel had earlier attempted to deconstruct— continue to be a decisive force in twentieth century politics: "They would never have dropped such a bomb on a white nation" (p. 286). He strips the insignia off his uniform and rides his motorcycle in a reversal of the route taken by the allied invasion of Italy. After the accident on the bridge, his descent into and re-emergence from the Ofanto river signals the re-birth of his identity as Kirpal Singh. He resumes the family tradition of the second son becoming a doctor, and the final pages depict not the relativizing of cultures but the affirmation of a racially-based Indian culture being lived in Kirpal Singh's family life: "At this table, all of their hands are brown. They move with ease in their customs and habits" (p. 301).

THE BODY AS SITE OF RESISTANCE

The central image of *The English Patient* is a figure whose identity is physically erased, made up of composite cultural influences and continually resistant to final definition. The one area of the novel where identity *is* presented in essentialist terms is in those passages which celebrate the body in a "euphoric appreciation of the here and now," as Bill Fledderus puts it: Hana's childlike delight in a game of hopscotch; her acrobatic hide and seek with Kip and Caravaggio; the dancing in the patient's room. At such moments, the ex-centric subjects leave their marginal existence and come into triumphant possession of themselves: "Kip seems unconsciously in love with his own body, with his physicalness, bending to pick up a slice of bread, his knuckles brushing the glass . . ." (p. 75). From his earliest works, particularly *The Collected Works of Billy the Kid*, Ondaatje seems to have shared Michel Foucault's view that the body is "directly involved in a political field; power relations have an immediate hold upon it; they invest it, mark it, train it, torture it, force it to carry out tasks, to perform ceremonies, to emit signs" (Foucault, p. 173). Foucault's account of the body as a political field is given a colonial dimension in Kip's description of army recruitment in British India, where the young men are wrested from their indigenous identity and, marked with yellow chalk, become signifiers in a military discourse whose end is power and violence (pp. 99–200).

In the context of war, the body is shown to be subjected to a range of technologies of control. There is the Gestapo photographing and archiving faces, as the character Bellocq does in *Coming Through Slaughter*. Mutilation is ubiquitous in *The English Patient* — from outside as when the Germans amputate Caravaggio's thumbs destroying his identity as a thief, or from internal pressures produced by the trauma of war, when Hana cuts short her hair, or others "break the way a man dismantling a mine broke the second his geography exploded. The way Hana broke when . . . an official . . . gave her a letter that told her of the death of her father" (41).

However, the body can also be a site of resistance. Caravaggio had appeared in *In the Skin of A Lion* as a figure who demonstrates his body's subversive energy through feats of acrobatic and sexual prowess. As Karen Overbye suggests, he is one of the characters for whom the body is an extension of the mind and self, and in *The English Patient* the scene in which he steals his photograph from the German officer's mistress offers an opportunity to celebrate the body's potency before its mutilation by the obscene technologies of war:

He ambles naked up the stairs to the second floor, where the guards are . . . So a long theatrical walk, and Caravaggio now having to perform it . . . the ass-and-cock walk, pausing at a section of mural to peer at a painted donkey in a grove. (pp. 37–8)

The swaggering delight in his sexuality gives him an inviolability; later, as cat burglar in the room with the fornicating general and his mistress, Caravaggio's trained body, its movements honed to balletic discipline, eludes the collective power of the Wehrmacht. As Overbye notes in relation to *In the Skin of A Lion*, Ondaatje is interested in the body as an agent of change and as the *bearer* of meaning rather than as passive recipient of society's inscriptions. In his novels bodies are inscribed not just by the state but by lovers themselves. In *In the Skin of A Lion*, at Caravaggio's imagined reunion with his wife, "[s]he pins the earring her fingers had strayed upon into his arm muscle, beginning a tatoo of blood" (p. 205), and Clara and Alice draw "a cave mural," "a spirit painting" on the body of the sleeping Patrick. There are parallels with scenes in *The*

English Patient: the sexual passion between Katharine and Almásy is recorded by a "list of wounds" (p. 153), bandages, bruises, iodine, just as, in The Cave of Swimmers, he transforms Katharine from her habitual self into a more timeless figure, "The ochre went into her face, he daubed blue around her eyes . . . There were traditions he had discovered in Herodotus in which old warriors celebrated their loved ones by locating and holding them in whatever world made them eternal — a colourful fluid, a song, a rock drawing" (p. 248). In *The English Patient* as in *In the Skin of A Lion*, the body is the site of very different forms of semiotic exchange: labelled, photographed, mutilated, the body is objectified in the interest of the state; but there is another kind of marking, in which inscription is not an instrument of power-knowledge, but part of a necessary exchange in which an individual loses his or her previous self and finds a new identity through relationship with another.

MASCULINITY, SEXUAL DESIRE AND IDENTITY

In Ondaatje's work, masculinity and sexual desire have been the field for his most complex exploration of the politics of identity. His poem, "White Dwarfs," is the key locus of these ideas, displaying a fascination for what Lorraine York calls "the male chaotic," for men whose violent creative energy liberates them from social constraints on identity and perception. However, as Ondaatje developed he came to value communal solidarity over the intense private vision of the outsider.

Almásy would seem to be an avatar of the violent artist of the earlier works — his breaking of a glass in a restaurant, and punching the glass of the cockpit a characteristic signature of the male hero's defiance of social law and principles of order. However, if in the retrospective passages dealing with Cairo society, Almásy represents the Romantic iconoclast, he increasingly becomes part of a network of relationships in the villa, which share a *collective* vision of the suffering of war being a product of global domination by "trade and power." Susan Ellis suggests that Almásy's development corresponds to a shift from Ondaatje's earlier valorization of an extreme masculinity. She relates this to the masculine self's need to differentiate itself from the mother by asserting an exteme individualism in contrast to feminine notions of the self which are founded on relationship. As iconoclast and loner in Cairo society, Almásy's improprieties carry a subversive appeal, but he moves beyond "his old desire for self-sufficiency" to recognize in the Villa's widening network of sympathies more productive forms of resistance.

The masculine self's need for differentiation is, in Kip's case, enhanced by his position as racial outsider, but Hana comes to resent the self-sufficiency in him, and in their sexual embraces Kip learns that to sacrifice isolation and surrender self-control may be the basis of a fuller identity gained through relatedness. Increasingly, we see Kip entering into networks of relationship, organizing the snailshell lights for Hana's birthday celebration at the Villa, and in the epilogue accepting his social and domestic ties as doctor and father in a Punjabi village.

In his earlier works, *Billy the Kid*, *Coming Through Slaughter*, and the poem "Peter," Ondaatje's fascination with male violence positioned women as passive victims, but, as Lorraine York suggests, there is evidence of a reassessment of gender in his later writing. It is certainly true that when Almásy's passion announces itself to Katharine in her dream, it does so in a disturbing violence to the passive female: "he had yoked her head back so she had been unable to breathe in her arousal." (149). However, in the Clifton-Katharine-Almásy and the Hana-Kip relationships, there is evidence of a re-evaluation of male sexuality, specifically in relation to notions of ownership, naming and an increasing recognition of the independence of women.

Quite clearly, the territorial possessiveness of the European cartographers, shown in their obsession with naming, finds a counterpart in the sexual possessiveness of the representative Imperial male, Clifton. Ostentatiously, Clifton brings his new plane and his new wife to the group of explorers, and his propensity to name and so to domesticate the alien—"I name this site the Bir Messaha Country Club." (p. 142) "He had named his plane *Rupert Bear*" (p. 143)— extends to the proprietorial language with which he describes his wife's body—"He celebrated the beauty of her arms, the thin lines of her ankles. He described witnessing her swim" (p. 230). From the beginnings of English colonialism, of course, sexual and territorial discovery and possession have been archly equated by the British male, and the Cliftons' concern with genealogy—"He had a family genealogy going back to Canute." (p. 237). "Just as she loved family traditions . . . She would have hated to die without a name. For her there was a line going back to her ancestors that was tactile, whereas [Almásy] had erased the path he had emerged from." (p. 170)—shows the need to appropriate the body and sexual procreation in a linear narrative that confers ownership on dominant class, race and gender, much as the names on maps confer exclusive ownership of land. By contrast, Almásy hates names, seeing in the act of naming a strategy by which nations and families incorporate individuals into structures of language and narratives of identity: "Erase the family name! Erase nations! I was taught such things by the desert . . . But I wanted to erase my name and the place I had come from" (p. 139).

Ultimately, the affair ends because Almásy's rejection of ownership and naming seems to Katharine an evasion of commitment and the social basis of relationship: "You slide past everything with your fear and hate of ownership, of owning, of being owned, of being named. You think this is a virtue. I think you are inhuman" (p. 238). While the denial of origins is in keeping with Ondaatje's frequently expressed sympathy for the outsider, there is a selfishness and sterility in Almásy's refusal to acknowledge relational ties (shown after the plane crash, when his failure to give Katharine's married name to the British soldiers ensures her death). It compares unfavorably with Katharine's organic rootedness in a network of kin and in a filiative tradition going back many generations — much like the one that Ondaatje was pleased to discover when he returned to Sri Lanka and found generations of his family name in the records of a Colombo church (see *Running in the Family*, pp. 22, 26).

The issue of sexual desire and identity is explored through the contrasting relationships of Almásy and Katharine, and Hana and Kip. The violence of Almásy's passion for Katharine is partly attributable to his need to wrest her from social controls and reach a self that is outside the stereotypes of class and gender, outside the social conditioning of the past: "The new lover enters the habits of the other. Things are smashed and revealed in new light. . . . A love story is not about those who lose their heart but about those who find that sullen inhabitant who, when it is stumbled upon, means the body can fool no one, can fool nothing — not the wisdom of sleep or the habit of social graces. It is a consuming of oneself and the past" (p. 97). As "an organ of fire", the heart's desire "burn[s] down all social rules," leaving Almásy "disassembled," "manic[ally]" intent on tearing Katharine "from within the walls of her class" (p. 155). Awesome in its power, the desire that breaks down all boundaries of identity, all definitions of the self can find no final ground of relationship, since its quest is for an object beyond the defining limits of "character" (p. 173).

Almásy and Katharine's relationship — based on a disassembling of social selves — is counterbalanced by the relationship between the

Canadian Hana and the Sikh Kip. In a novel where demarcations of geography, architecture, race and body are continually being broken down, Kip is notable for his ability to hold on to his private space. In contrast to Almásy and Katharine, the relationship of Hana and Kip preserves the integrity of their separate selves: "Revealing his past or qualities of his character would have been too loud a gesture. Just as he could never turn and enquire of her what deepest motive caused this relationship" (197). Their embraces bring, not a dissolution of identity, but a confirmation of selfhood through a non-dominative encounter with the racial other: "She imagines all of Asia through the gestures of this man . . . At night when she lets his hair fall free, he is once more another constellation . . . She holds an Indian goddess in her arms, she holds wheat and ribbons" (pp. 217–8). In contrast to the narcissism of the colonizer who, in relation to the other, merely wishes to see "a graven image of himself" (p. 142), and in contrast to Almásy's possessiveness towards Katharine, Hana and Kip offer a relationship based not on domination but intersubjectivity, a mutual respect for the integrity of the other.

In his early works, Ondaatje tends to establish the violent energy of his heroes through the portrayal of women as passive victims of masculine power. In *The English Patient*, too, the intensity of Almásy's relationship with Katharine is first shown through an image of violence to the female body, and there are other such disturbing images, of women tethered to their men by a leash around the little finger, of the small Arab girl tied up in Fenelon Barnes' bed. As Lorraine York suggests, however, "there is some rethinking of the commodification of women going on in Ondaatje's poems and novels" (York, p. 80), and this particularly relates to the activity of looking and being looked at. For Clifton and Almásy, viewing is a vehicle of control and ownership: "[Clifton] celebrated the beauty of of her arms, the thin line of her ankles. He described witnessing

her swim" (p. 230). Almásy associates viewing with the first appro-
priative gaze of man on woman, "I see her still, always, with the eye
of Adam." (p. 144), but later he finds himself the object of a
woman's gaze: "All these years I have been trying to unearth what
she was handing me with that look . . . Now I think she was studying
me" (p. 144). There is a similar reversal of subject-object positions
in a scene involving Hana and Caravaggio: "He turns and sees Hana
asleep on the sofa . . . He sneezed out loud, and . . . She was awake,
the eyes staring ahead of him" (p. 81). In the course of the novel,
Katharine rejects the female role of victim by striking Almásy vio-
lently, while Hana rejects chaste passivity by initiating sexual relations with Kip. Such assertions of female autonomy are related to
the novel's wider questioning of subject-object positions within the
power structures it depicts.

MAPPING, SPATIAL BOUNDARIES

The theme of ex-centricity in *The English Patient* finds its most
overt political expression in the novel's handling of the map *topos*.
In his article, "Theorising Post-Colonial Space," Richard Cavell has
argued that the "enterprise of colonialism has a fundamentally spa-
tial aspect, the seizing of territories, the mapping of sights, construction and demolition of buildings" (p. 111). According to J. Hillis
Miller, "The power of the conventions of mapping . . . [is] so great
that we see the landscape as if it is already a map, complete with
place names and the names of geographical features. The place
names seem to be intrinsic to the places they name" (Hillis Miller,
quoted in Jacobs, p. 3). The appearance of naturalness and objectiv-
ity, however, of conveying meanings that are already immanent in
the landscape, masks the function of maps as representations of
space that suit particular interests and projects. The naming of

places and features grants title and controlling knowledge.
lonial fiction differs from colonial in its more critical awarei
the role of mapping in the history of Empire. Ondaatje hac
the importance of mapping in relation to his own experience of
colonialism. In *Running in the Family*, the narrator describes Ceylon as a territory for foreign cartographers serving the powerful
interests of invaders and traders. Significantly, one of *The English
Patient's* most important intertexts is Kipling's *Kim*, a novel about
colonial India in which mapping is seen as essential to Britain's
control of the subcontinent.

The English patient himself is based on the historical Count
Almásy, a Hungarian who was part of a group of European explorers
mapping the Libyan desert in the 1920s and 1930s. In the novel,
however, Almásy comes to see mapping as an instrument of colonial
domination.

The ends of the earth are never the points on a map that colonists push
against, enlarging their sphere of influence. On one side servants and slaves
and tides of power and correspondence with the Geographical Society. On
the other the first step by a white man across a great river, the first sight (by
a white eye) of a mountain that has been there forever. (p. 141)

Almásy sees mapping as a form of knowledge through which power
extends its dominion, establishing oppressive structures of class
("servants") and race ("slaves") in new lands. In contrast to a hum-
bling encounter with the other, whether mountain or great river,
the colonial mentality is narcissistic, projecting its own identity onto
the alien landscape — "Narcissus wants a graven image of himself"
(p. 142). However, as Graham Huggan argues, maps have an ambiguous role in postcolonial texts. While maps can function as visual
analogues for colonialism and its imposition of fixed meanings on
territory, some postcolonial texts undermine colonial discourse by

envisioning the map as simply one of many versions of territory offered by different cultures—rather than as the representation of a literal truth. It is precisely in these terms that Almásy's review of desert cartography unfixes the rigid definitions through which the territorial claims of Europe are advanced:

The desert could not be claimed or owned—it was a piece of cloth carried by winds, never held down by stones, and given a hundred shifting names before Canterbury had existed, long before battles and treaties had quilted Europe and the East. (p. 139)

Colonialism and neo-colonialism tend to be oblivious of the *social* construction of space, the fact that space is invariably lived in, worked by particular people and that it acquires meaning and significance in relation to specific human needs and experiences. Richard Cavell notes that it is a feature of neo-colonial discourse in Canada to treat space as "an abstraction that denies the social dimension" (Cavell, p. 112). It is precisely against an impulse of this kind, to reify space by inscribing it with fixed meanings, that the English patient recalls the *history* of maps and the specific social projects that motivated them:

So history enters us. I knew maps of the sea floor, maps that depict weaknesses in the shield of the earth, charts painted on skin that contain the various routes of the Crusades. So I knew their place before I crashed among them, knew when Alexander had traversed it in an earlier age, for this cause or that greed. I knew the customs of nomads besotted by silk or wells. (p. 18)

By presenting space as subject to conflicting territorial projects, the English patient recovers the social history denied in colonial cartographers' attempt to present their maps as neutral and objective. By drawing attention to the materiality and aesthetic quality of maps, he denies them transparency as signs that merely reflect a meaning that is intrinsic in the landscape.

The map *topos* is part of a wider interest in the organization of space in *The English Patient*, which can be linked to its critique of the power structures inherent in colonialism. The novel's evocation of setting undermines the ways in which societies conventionally impose forms and meanings on space,

There seemed little demarcation between house and landscape, between damaged building and the burned and shelled remnants of the earth. To Hana the wild gardens were like further rooms. (p. 43)

Such passages break down conventional hierarchies and divisions, such as between outside and inside, bedroom and library, and disrupt the clear relation between architectural form and function — as in Hana's habit of converting domestic spaces into her bedroom by fixing her hammock to the walls. The imperial conception of space assumes the perspective of a sovereign eye from which meaning, order, intelligibility can be conferred, but as Mark Simpson has suggested (Simpson, p. 217), the Villa San Girolamo is characterized by tropes of illegibility. The books Hana reads the English patient have gaps of plot in them and "The villa which she and the Englishman inhabited now was much like that" (p. 8).

POSTMODERNISM, HISTORY AND *THE ENGLISH PATIENT*

The significance of postmodernism in the Canadian culture which Ondaatje became part of in the 1960s has been considered in the introductory section above. Postmodernism shows a distrust of dominant narratives of the past, and as I. Maver suggests, this has made it particularly suited to the Canadian cultural context, which is "characterized by pluralism, decentralization and the creation of a multi-cultural 'mosaic' " (Maver, p. 65). The 1960s were a period in which Anglo-Canadian accounts of Canadian history and national identity were being challenged by writers from previously marginalized perspectives, and Ondaatje's awareness of his own cultural hybridity, of possessing the migrant's "double perspective" made it natural for him to sympathize with these impulses. Postmodernist poetics are above all characterized by formal strategies that recognize and celebrate pluralism and decentralization, and one of the most significant of these strategies is the postmodern representation of history.

Postmodernist writers in Canada have shown a particular concern with history, with challenging official versions of the past by problematizing the relation between history and fiction. This has linked them with a distinctive novel genre, historiographic metafiction:

However, it is this very separation of the literary and the historical that is now being challenged in postmodern theory and art, and recent critical readings of both history and fiction have focused more on what the two modes of writing share than on how they differ. They have both been seen to derive their force more from verisimilitude than from any objective truth; they are both identified as linguistic constructs, highly conventionalised in their narrative forms, and not all transparent either in terms of language or structure. (L. Hutcheon, *A Poetics of Postmodernism*, p. 105)

Historiographic metafictions "both install and blur the line between fiction and history" (ibid. p. 113). These novels seem to be part of historical discourse, but at the same time they proclaim their status as fiction. Similarly, they make use of the conventions of realism only to parody them, and thus expose the claims of such literature to give direct access to objective truth. A number of Canadian postmodern novels explore the conflict between oral and written records. The oral mode is based on "gossip and communal (mythic) memory," and is "tied to myth, legend and fairy story and the fanciful imagination of the tall tale," while "the written one is linked instead to the cause-and-effect rationality and realism of the historical narrative" (L. Hutcheon, *The Canadian Postmodern*, p. 53). Postmodern novels explore the tension between the two to question the accepted hierarchy of factual record over oral memory. While Almásy's written diary record dominates the novel, its ending anticipates Katherine's assimilation into communal, oral memory: "We are communal histories, communal books . . . I carried Katharine Clifton into the desert, where there is the communal book of moonlight. We were among *the rumour* of wells" (p. 261, my italics).

The central role of Herodotus shows the importance of history in *The English Patient* and the novel illustrates the typical postmodern concern to question history's supposedly authoritative version of the past. As a historian, Herodotus poses the distinctively postmodern question about how history is related to fiction, and the difficulty of distinguishing between fact and fiction, something which the Western tradition has cared not to recognize. Herodotus' *History* becomes a model of the way in which "history" is reconstructed in the novel:

I see him more as one of those spare men of the desert who travel from oasis to oasis, trading legends as if it is the exchange of seeds, consuming everything without suspicion, piecing together a mirage. "This history of mine," Herodotus says, "has from the beginning sought out the supplementary to the main argument." What you find in him are cul-de-sacs within the sweep of history—how people betray each other for the sake of nations, how people fall in love. . . . (pp. 118–9)

Called both "the father of history" and "the father of lies," Herodotus' sources were predominantly oral—stories and reports from soldiers who had fought in the Persian wars, from Athenian and Spartan family traditions, from priests and other men at Delphi or in Egypt. What modern historians accept as accurate record co-exists with the fabulous as in the account of giant ants digging up sand with a rich content of gold, and such accounts are frequently accompanied by a sceptical disclaimer, "There is a story about the Phoenix . . . such at least is the story" (p. 157), "such at least are the reports on how these people live" (p. 12), "I merely repeat the tradition . . ." (p. 272). What these illustrate is a persistent instability in the evidentiary status of the narrative of the *Histories*, and the rejection of a single authoritative version of the past in favor of a record of the multiple voices that constitute a communal, oral record. There is a similar instability in *The English Patient*, where passages in the mode of the classical historical novel—"It was not until 1940 that the War Office took over bomb disposal, and then, in turn, handed it over to the Royal Engineers" (p. 182)—contrast with the English patient's handwritten narrative which draws on the memory bank of oral tradition often drawn from Herodotus (e.g., pp. 16–17). Almásy's use of Herodotus in his researches on the desert again points up the problematic relation between truth and fiction in historical discourse:

His only connection with the world of cities was Herodotus, his guidebook, ancient and modern, of supposed lies. When he discovered the truth to what had seemed a lie, he brought out his glue pot and pasted in a map or news clipping or used a blank page in the book to sketch men in skirts with faded unknown animals alongside them. (p. 246)

The main narrative of *The Histories* concerns the establishment of the Persian Empire and the Greek city states' resistance to the imperial yoke, which parallels the account of Indian resistance to the British Empire in *The English Patient*. Herodotus frequently interrupts his main narrative with a multitude of subplots. Some of these, such as the Gyges and Candaules episode, or that involving Ariston and Agetus' wife, involve sexual betrayal, while others narrate the betrayal of one's own side to the enemy, as in the account of Euphorbus and Philagrus. These plot motifs are paralleled in Almásy's betrayal of Clifton and of the allies to the Germans.

Herodotus' *History* is above all concerned with the establishment and destruction of national and imperial boundaries — the gradual extension of the Persian empire into Europe and Asia Minor, followed by its defeat, the foundation of the Greek City states, Athens and Sparta. As an ethnologist, Herodotus also shows a preoccupation with the basis of ethnic identity — "Having described the various resources of [Scythia], I will go on to give some account of the people's customs and beliefs" (p. 289). He provides a perspective on the transience of empire and of national and cultural identities, which in *The English Patient* is set against the grandiose claims of imperial power in the twentieth century: "We knew power and great finance were temporary things. We all slept with Herodotus. *'For those cities that were great in earlier times must have now become small, and those that were great in my time were small in the time before . . .'*" (p. 142, quoting *The Histories* I, vii).

The English Patient draws on a number of historical sources — for example, in the passages on the history of bomb disposal and in the characters of Almásy and the Cliftons. Critics have noted that Ondaatje frequently incoporates marginal figures from history into his fiction. As Stephen Tostoy de Zepetnek shows, Almásy's identity proves to be elusive in the historical sources also, which provide contradictory accounts of his aristocratic status — "Who was this

Count Almásy?", writes Buckheit, the historian (de Zepetnek, p. 145). There is a mysterious quality about the original Almásy which corresponds with his role in the novel. By making this shadowy figure the hero of his novel, Ondaatje reverses the centre/margin relationship obtaining in conventional histories. However, the force of Ondaatje's use of actual historical figures derives from the tension he creates between two régimes of truth to which his characters belong, between what Ondaatje calls "the truth of fiction" and the truth of history. Aspects of Almásy are based on historical records—the discovery of the lost oasis of Zerzura in the Libyan desert and of the cave paintings in the Uweinat mountains, the mapping of the Libyan desert, his espionage work for Rommel, his book on desert exploration. Ondaatje's combination of the historical and the fictional exemplifies a characteristic strategy of postmodernist fiction, the use of "the doubled referent." The characters and situations of *The English Patient* refer to two different realities, one historical and one literary, and the shifts between the two effect a blurring of the distinction between fact and fiction.

In an interview with Eleanor Wachtel, Ondaatje explained the origins of *The English Patient*, and, in particular, the significance of the desert and Herodotus:

> . . . once I got into the desert stuff, and through that to Herodotus, I began picking up a sense of the layers of history. I was going back deeper and deeper in time. There are churches in Rome that stand on the remains of two or three earlier churches, all built on the same spot. That sense of history, of building overlaid with building was central in my mind—unconsciously I think. (Wachtel, p. 251)

The English Patient rejects the conception of history as founded on a single linear narrative in favour of a sense of the multiple strata of the past that can be found in one location. Searching for Zerzura in the 1930s, Almásy is aware of earlier expeditions, the Zenussi raid of the Great War, Williamson in 1838, and Cambyses' lost army in the Fifth Century B.C. (pp. 138–40). Similarly, he decides that the Villa San Girolamo was originally the Villa Bruscoli belonging to the Renaissance poet, Poliziano, and the center for a rich Renaissance culture with contemporary artists, philosophers and cartographers, Michaelangelo, Pico della Mirandola, Toscanelli in attendance. His account of Savanorola destroying this rich civilization with fire (p. 57) carries a strong parallel with the World War II narrative in *The English Patient,* which describes how the civilization of the West culminates in all-consuming nuclear holocaust: "If he closes his eyes he sees the streets of Asia full of fire. It rolls across the cities like a burst map . . . This tremor of Western wisdom." (pp. 283–4)

The narrative of Renaissance Italy repeats itself in the mid-twentieth century, and this is also a feature of historiographic metafiction, in which history is seen to be based on plots that seem be able to reproduce themselves independently in different contexts. Almásy comments on the problems encountered by the allied army in its advance into Northern Italy: ". . . the Germans have barracked themselves into villas and convents and they are brilliantly defended. *It's an old story* — the Crusaders made the same mistake against the Saracens. And like them you need the fortress towns" (p. 96, my italics). The past is seen as being textualised as plot, a story which has the uncanny ability to repeat itself in the present.

INTERTEXTUALITY

The interrogation of the boundary between history and fiction, and the challenge to history's claim to provide access to objective truth have both invoked the concept of "intertextuality." Intertextuality challenges the assumption that the author is sole source of the text's meaning by locating the source of a text's meaning in past discourses. Any particular text will derive its narrative structures, themes, models of character in part from previous texts. Works regarded as historiographic metafiction make frequent allusions to artistic, historical and literary texts in order to show the extent to which both literary and historical works are dependent on the history of discourse. Hutcheon argues in *The Canadian Postmodern* that Canadian fiction is characterized by the parodic use of traditional forms and conventions — biblical narratives, or narratives of quest. The irony and distance involved in parody allows the text to separate itself from the original while recognizing its complicity with it.

The English Patient is notable for the number and scope of its intertexts, which range from works that supply an overarching structure for the novel to those which provide a more local elucidation of theme: Kipling's *Kim*, Milton's *Paradise Lost*, the Gyges-Candaules episode in Herodotus, *The Tempest*, *Anna Karenina*, *The Charterhouse of Parma*, Caravaggio's painting of David, the Grail legend. The last of these, though one of the least explicitly acknowledged, is structurally the most important of the intertexts. In his article, "The English Patient lay in his bed like a [Fisher] King," Bill Fledderus provides a detailed study of the links between the novel and the Grail legends, and my discussion that follows is indebted to his researches.

Though there is no explicit reference to the Grail legends or ancient fertility cults in *The English Patient*, a reader acquainted (as Ondaatje was) with Eliot's use of this mythic material in *The Waste Land* would recognize familiar patterns. The Fisher King is found in a number of fertility myths. His land is ravaged and he himself is maimed and impotent. The curse is lifted with the arrival of a knight who must successfully undergo certain trials, sometimes aided by the Grail maiden. Once he has done this, fertility is restored to the land.

In *The English* Patient, the mediaeval context of the Grail is evoked though numerous references to knights, and the similarity between "the destroyed chapel" of the villa and Eliot's "empty chapel" in *The Waste Land*. The fertility myths and the Grail legend offer the pattern of sterility and desolation followed by re-newal of life and fertility. The novel's use of the motif of sterility provides an implicit commentary on the physical and spiritual state of a war-torn Europe. As Fledderus shows, the figure of the English patient has a number of resemblances to the Fisher King: he is maimed by burns which are most severe in the region of the thigh, the location of the Fisher King's wound; he is associated with impotence; a number of Grail romances describe a dead knight lying on an altar in a candlelit room, a motif associated with the English patient; in the Grail romances, the wounding and impo-tence of the Fisher King is mirrored in the ravaging and sterility of the land, and this is of course a feature of the architecture and landscape of the Villa setting; at times, such descriptions hint at a more generalised, Eliotesque state of desolation and sterility: ". . . between damaged building and the shelled remnants of the earth . . . In spite of the burned earth, in spite of the lack of water" (p. 43). In the Grail Romances, the state of the land is attributed to political and sexual-moral guilt, and in the novel the patient recognizes his complicity with the forces that have brought destruction—"This country—had I charted it and turned it into a place of war?" (p. 260)—while his adultery is an example of sexual guilt.

Kip would correspond to the figure of Perceval in the Grail. Perceval is the knight traveller who comes upon the Fisher King, and by performing a feat restores the king and the land. In the novel, Kip is associated with warrior saints and is pictured as the travelling knight (p. 273). The patient regards him as "my younger self.". Kip attempts to save the land by removing bombs from it, and in a context strongly suggestive of ruin and decay, he is notably connected with a renewal of life and fertility — "She holds wheat and ribbons. As he bends over her it pours" (p. 218). Perceval is trained by an isolated knight, parallelling Lord Suffolk's training of Kip; they both have experiences in chapels, and perform similar heroic feats.

Hana shares features with a number of women who appear in the Romances. She is like the lamenting women that Perceval finds attending the Fisher King. The cutting of hair is associated with a number of fertility rituals. Hana's shorn hair seems to represent the failure of earlier relationships with men, symbolized by the aborted child, and her response to the prevalence of death during the war, including that of her own father. After her relationship with Kip — his long hair imaging vitality — her hair grows and children are born (though not to her). Hana's attributes link her to the Fertility Queen of the Grail Romances — her gardening in the wasted soil, her position by the fountain at the moment when "there is a crash as the water arrives bursting around her" (p. 92); the communal birthday meal given a ritualistic quality by the candlelight made from snail shells (p. 267).

The English Patient reflects the postmodernist insight that experience in the present is determined by what Roland Barthes calls "the infinite text" — "I am a person who . . . pulls down a volume and inhales it. So history enters us" (p. 18). Narratives from the past, whether from history, as in the case of the Crusaders, or from literature and oral culture structure the events and relationships of the present. The Gyges-Candaules episode from Herodotus motivates Almásy's affair with Katharine Clifton. The story of the king whose boasts about his wife's beauty provoke her adultery and his own death is recited by Katharine and arouses Almásy's desire for her: "with the help of an anecdote, I fell in love. Words, Caravaggio.

They have a power" (p. 235). But the novel eschews any simple equivalence between text and intertext: thus Hana is both Grail maiden and "Squire," saint and seductress; if Almásy is Gyges and Katharine is Candaules' wife, the role of murderer fits Clifton who tries to kill all of them with his plane, and it is Caravaggio who is seen naked by the German officer's mistress. The intertext provides a structural matrix whose elements are recast as beguiling traces that can be directed in all kinds of narrative bye-ways. David Roxburgh has explored the extensive parallels that exist between *The English Patient* and images, figures, settings from the Bible. He concludes that "Ondaatje's system of myth is 'imagistic' not allegorical, and transient connections exist only long enough for the reader to notice their significance" (Roxburgh, p. 243). He agrees with Joseph Pesch that the function of the mythic material is to satisfy the reader's "nostalgic longing for pre-apocalyptic stability" (Pesch, p. 119), and to provide a "cohesive clarity lacking in the novel's fragmented and ambiguous action" (Roxburgh, p. 240). As he shows, the novel can also adopt an ironic, critical relation to the texts to which it alludes.

Rudyard Kipling's *Kim* is a text given particular attention in *The English Patient*. Kip's name is phonetically similar to the English author and his novel. Hana quotes passages from it at several points and wonders how the central characters of Kipling's novel might be paralleled in herself, Kip and the patient. *Kim* is set in India at the end of the Nineteenth Century. It is the story of an orphan boy of Irish descent, Kim, who follows a Tibetan lama on a journey from Lahore across India in a quest for wisdom. In the course of the journey, he becomes involved in espionage, and is recruited by the British officer Creighton, who educates him in schools based on the English model. There is a rich and complex parallelism between *The English Patient* and its Kipling intertext. Most obviously, there is a reversal of the situation in *Kim*, with the young Indian sitting at the feet of the European sage. The central irony consists in the different forms of wisdom gained by the young disciples. The lama's oriental wisdom involves a serene renunciaton of "the Wheel," the things of the world, but in *The English Patient*, "this tremor of Western wisdom" issues in a holocaust that destroys the world.

Kim is an example of what Edward Said (1978) has defined as Orientalism, a style of thought which assumes, as a fundamental ground of knowledge and reality, that there is a distinction between the Orient and the Occident: "the basic distinction between East and West [is] the starting point for theories, epics, novels, social descriptions, and political accounts concerning the Orient, its people, customs, 'mind', destiny and so on" (Said, pp. 2–3). Furthermore, Orientalism adopts a "positional superiority" of West over East, and it is therefore in Michel Foucault's sense a *discourse*, a system of knowledge that organizes its material in such a way as to exercise power and control. It is precisely such a form of knowledge that is repeatedly vaunted in *Kim*: ". . . even an Oriental, with an Oriental's view of the value of time. . . . Kim could lie like an Oriental" (p. 33). Creighton is, like Almásy, an ethnologist and geographer, who shows a sympathetic understanding of Indian customs, language and religion, but his knowledge is shown to be a vital instrument of political control. *Kim* is implicated in the discourse of colonialism, and this explains the significance of the passage in which Hana records, in the margins of Kipling's novel, Kip's account of the history of Lahore. In this and subsequent passages, we have what Said terms a "contrapuntal" narrative, the voice of the Oriental giving his own version of Indian history, customs and politics. It is a version that celebrates a heroic past and a present of resistance to colonial oppression, and it is very different from the kind of knowledge associated with the idealised figure of the lama in Kipling's novel, whose wisdom involves a renunciation of "the Wheel," the world, leaving it to be fought over by rival Imperial powers.

One of the passages from *Kim* read out by Hana ends: *"In a minute — in another half second — he felt he would arrive at the solution of the tremendous puzzle . . ."* (*EP*, p. 111, italics in original). The nature of the puzzle is made clear if one looks at the paragraph before in Kipling:

A very few white people, but many Asiatics, can throw themselves into amazement as it were by repeating their own names over and over again to themselves, letting the mind go free upon speculation as to what is called personal identity. When one grows older, the power usually departs, but while it lasts it may descend upon a man at any moment. "Who is Kim. — Kim — Kim?" (*Kim*, pp. 264–5)

The problem of identity is central to Kipling's novel, as it is to *The English Patient*. In particular, the theme of hybridity recurs in Ondaatje's interviews, his family biography, and in the figure of Kip who — in a process of reverse colonization — assimilates and mimics English customs and values as Kim does Indian ones. Kipling's novel shows that problems of identity are not simply experienced by colonized but by colonizer. Kim's identity is in continual transformation as he changes his clothing and skin colour from Hindu to Mohammedan, to Eurasian, to English, and he is able to mimic the language appropriate to these identities, and so reveal the extent to which they are cultural constructs rather than innate. Like the English patient, Kim's elusive identity is figured in his skin — he is "white, a poor white," though *"burned black"* (my italics), the son of an Irish colour sergeant (one of the colonized who has taken on the role of colonizer). One of his projects in the novel is to reclaim his birthright and to define his identity —

All that while he felt . . . that his soul was out of gear with its surroundings—
a cog-wheel unconnected with any machinery . . . I am Kim. I am Kim.
And what is Kim?(p. 403)—

and it is a similar process of self-discovery that Kip is engaged in at
the end of *The English Patient* in passages that carry a verbal echo
of *Kim*—compare "His name is Kirpal Singh and he does not know
what he is doing here." (*EP*, p. 283) with ". . . by repeating their
own names over and over again. . . . 'Who is Kim—Kim—Kim?' "
(*Kim*, p. 264). Ondaatje chooses to quote a passage from *Kim* that
is of particular significance for postcolonial identity politics. While
Kipling's text can be read as a classic defence of British colonialism
in India, the quoted extract shows that it is troubled by questions of
identity and these extend to questions about the meaning of the
British role in India, "a cog-wheel unconnected with any machinery." Ondaatje's use of the Kipling intertext, therefore, involves a
subtle subversion of its ideological intent.

VARIETIES OF GENRE AND LANGUAGES

Intertextuality and parody are related to another feature of postmodernist fiction, the crossing of generic boundaries. Genre can be
defined as the set of expectations raised by a text as to how it is to
be read and what form of coherence is to be looked for. While a
text's adherence to genre will tend to confirm a reader's expectations
of coherence, the crossing of generic boundaries suggests that coherence is based on culturally specific formal conventions.

The Canadian writers' position on the periphery of the dominant
culture has encouraged them to explore the boundaries between
genres. Critics have noted Ondaatje's fascination with boundaries
and linked this with his defiance of the boundaries of literary genres.

Geetha Ganapathy-Dore's study of *The English Patient*, "The Novel of the Nowhere Man," relates Ondaatje's concern with the "international bastards," products of heterogeneous cultural influences, to his rejection of stylistic homogeneity and his exploitation of the diversity of genres and discourses which have always been a feature of the novel as a form. *The English Patient* includes elements of the historical novel, the colonial novel, the autobiographical memoir, the epistolary novel, the detective thriller, magical realism (Ganapathy-Dore, p. 99).

Ondaatje's work has always been characterized by its mixing of different discourses, newspaper article, popular song, comic strip. The different language systems compete with one another and no discourse is given ultimate authority—in a way that Fredric Jameson suggests is a defining feature of the postmodern condition, which has witnessed ". . . the stupendous proliferation of social codes today into professional and disciplinary jargons . . . If the ideas of a ruling class were once the dominant (or hegemonic) ideology of bourgeois society, the advanced capitalist countries today are now a field of stylistic and discursive heterogeneity without a norm" (Jameson, p. 17). In *The English Patient*, the diversity of styles and discourses employed in the narration includes: scientific; geographic; cartographic; military-technological; military slang; medical; logical positivist—*"If a man's life could be capitalized at X, the risk at Y, and the estimated damage from explosion at V, then a logician might contend. . . ."* (p. 212); historical; the voice of Renaissance culture and of the classicist; English gardening and ornithology; upperclass English—"Miss Morden is a splendid judge of character" (p. 189); Arab culture—"There are some European words you can never translate properly into another language. *Félhomály.* The dusk of graves" (p. 170); mediaevalism; erotic. The stylistic richness is enhanced by the frequent use of interpolated quotations from Herodotus, the Book of Isaiah, the songs of Gershwin and Lorenz Hart, the work of Tacitus, Kipling, Stephen Crane, Milton's *Paradise Lost*, Shakespeare, Tolstoy's *Anna Karenina*, Stendhal's *The Charterhouse of Palma*, extracts from historical works, records of the Royal Geographical Society.

The effect of such discursive variety is to present the reader with different and conflicting régimes of truth. In choosing a particular language, the individual chooses with it a particular way of perceiving and comprehending the world. The use of scientific language introduces an empirical perspective on reality and a utilitarian conception of value, which is contrasted with other perceptual modes — the aesthetic-religious response to the world evoked by quoting Adam's description of the stars in *Paradise Lost*, which is itself set against the word *félhomály* suggesting a perspective outside the Judaeo-Christian tradition. The novel's stylistic range thus has the effect of undermining unitary cognitive modes. Mikhail Bakhtin argued that the novel has, since its emergence as a form, been characterized by the heterogeneity of linguistic styles that it represents, by its *heteroglossia*. By mapping the linguistic strata that existed in a particular epoch, it was, according to Bakhtin, instrumental in forming national consciousness in Nineteenth Century Europe. *The English Patient* extends linguistic variety beyond national boundaries and could therefore be seen to contribute to a global consciousness. Cultural references to English gardens are juxtaposed with Arabic words and concepts; there are references to Judaeo-Christian, Sikh, Egyptian, Greek religious beliefs. Such heterogeneity embodies a syncretism that effectively suggests a late twentieth century, postnational cultural politics.

Critics have commented on the figurative density of the narrators' language in *The English Patient*, and Ondaatje himself has suggested in interview that much of his best poetry went into the writing of the novel. The narrators' descriptions make use of poetic conceits whose unexpectedness can force the reader to vizualise the scene with attentiveness and precision: "The First Canadian Infantry Division worked its way up Italy, and the destroyed bodies were fed back to the field hospitals like mud passed back by tunnellers in the dark" (p. 49); often there is a degree of excess that gives an element of self-display to the narrative voice: "So the books for the Englishman. . . . had gaps of plot like sections of road washed out by storms, missing incidents as if locusts had consumed a section of tapestry . . ." (p. 7); "[the birds in bamboo cages] appeared like brides in a mediaeval courtship" (p. 145); "He plucked a thread from the horde of nights and put it into his mouth like food" (p. 246). Such passages make a contrast with the photographic sequences providing a minute objective record. The transparency of the latter is opposed to the self-reflexive poetic passages where frequent and extravagant use of simile foregrounds linguistic medium over message. The novel, the dominant modern literary form of the West, has been defined by its "formal realism," one feature of which has been the transparency of the language it employs, which appears to give direct access to reality. Ondaatje's employment of poetic narration challenges an important formal convention of the novel genre. Furthermore, by emphasizing the aesthetic frame such passages point to the particular perspective and bias from which reality is being represented, and make it impossible for the reader to accept that representation as authoritative truth. The descriptions in *The English Patient* often have a surplus of sensuousness— "There is a boy dancing . . . His thin shoulders white as papyrus . . . nakedness glimpsed through openings in the blue linen he wears as a lure from neck to ankle, revealing himself as a line of brown lightning . . . everything drifted like the shift of linen across the boy as if he were embracing or freeing himself from the ocean or his own blue afterbirth." (p. 22)—similar to that attributed to the old Arab poet who compares an oasis to his woman's "white-dove shoulders" (p. 108), which suggests that the poetic style is partly intended to suggest an exotic way of apprehending the world different from the more utilitarian Western modes found elsewhere in the novel.

In its claim to provide a direct access to reality, the traditional realist novel has tended to suppress the communicating situation, or to make it appear natural. Postmodernist fiction, by contrast, has typically emphasized the enunciation, the process of the production of meaning. By continually shifting the position of speaker and listener, narrator and narratee, *The English Patient* prevents the reader from assuming that meaning derives from a stable centre. Furthermore, it draws attention to the physical and material medium involved in communication. The English patient forces Hana to attend to the *sound* of Kipling's prose: "Read him slowly, dear girl, you must read Kipling slowly. Watch carefully where the commas fall so you can discover the natural pauses. He is a writer who used pen and ink. He looked up from the page a lot . . . Think about the speed of his pen" (p. 94).

PLOT STRUCTURE AND POINT OF VIEW

The elements of intertextuality, parody and heterogeneity of style in postmodernist writing are, according to Fredric Jameson, linked to the end of the traditional concept of the autonomous subject with a firm center to its identity. Whereas traditional concepts of the subject assume a consciousness that is coherent and consistent over time, the "decentered subject" proposes a view of identity as discontinuous, as dispersed between the different cultural influences that constitute it. Clearly such a conception of the subject has important implications for the narrative structure and form of fiction influenced by it. Michel Foucault has argued that "Continuous history is the indispensable correlative of the founding function of the subject: the guarantee that everything that has eluded him may/ restored to him; the certainty that time will disperse nothing without restoring it in a reconstituted unity" (Foucault quoted by Hutcheon 1988, p. 158). Through their disruption of continuous linear sequence, the plots of postmodernist fiction typically challenge the concept of the stable unified subject.

Ondaatje's earlier fiction was characterized by its rejection of the simple linear plots of the traditional novel in favour of collage, the development of plot through fragments of narrative from multiple points of view. *The English Patient*, too, shows a resistance to strict causal logic and linear sequence. In an interview he gave at the time of writing the novel, Ondaatje said, "I don't believe stories are told from A to Z any more" (Wachtel, p. 254), and in a characteristically self-reflexive passage, "so the books for the Englishman . . . had gaps of plot" (p. 7), *The English Patient* draws attention to its own principles of construction. If the narrative emphasizes discontinuity, the function of Kip's expertise with bombs and the patient's encyclopaedic knowledge of history and geography is partly, as Rufus Cook suggests, to fill in "the 'gaps of plot,' of providing connection and continuity to an experience which, in itself, is inherently discontinuous" (Cook, p. 113).

In addition to rejecting linear progression, the novel presents the reader with multiple storylines. As a formal strategy, this continues the determination expressed in the epigraph to *In the Skin of A Lion* to challenge dominant versions of the past: "Never again will a single story be told as if it were the only one" (John Berger). *The English Patient* has passages in the mode of the traditional historical novel, in which an omniscient third person narrator provides an authoritative history of desert exploration, World War II bomb disposal and the allied campaign in Italy, but set against the voice of official history are the stories of Hana, the English patient, Caravaggio and Kip.

In discussing his methods of composition, Ondaatje has stressed the care with which he re-works the sequence of incidents and passages in his fiction, because of the importance he attaches to structure. The novel deals with a relatively short though unspecified present time: the initial situation of Hana nursing the patient followed by the arrival of Caravaggio, then Kip; the developing closeness between the four characters until the announcement of the nuclear bombing of Hiroshima and Nagasaki destroys the community established at the Villa. The narrative of the present is frequently interrupted by analepsis (flashback), giving each character's development. These vary from brief fragments to, in the case of Kip, full scale biographies, and they frequently do not follow in chronological sequence. In addition, there is rapid cutting between the different characters' pasts. Key information — such as Hana's loss of her baby, Kip's argument with his brother — is delayed. These strategies challenge the reader's construction of a stable model of character, and the novel rejects the concept of character as unified in favor of one that stresses the discontinuities in our grasp of individual identity. A feature of the narrative is its frequent employment of "scene," in which the time taken to narrate approximates to the duration of the incident being described: for example, Hana's game of hopscotch, Caravaggio's theft of the photograph, Kip carrying a ladybird from the field to Hana, the game of hide-and-seek between Kip, Hana, and Caravaggio. As in his earlier works, Ondaatje adopts the perspective of a camera tracking his characters, and there is a striking contrast between such passages and those with the broad historical sweep of "From 425 BC to the beginning of the twentieth century there is an averting of eyes [from the desert]" (p. 133). The different temporalities raise questions about the relative importance of the macroscopic and microscopic perspectives, challenging the assumed authority of the historical point of view, and, as in Ondaatje's earlier works, attaching particular importance to an intense physical experience of the here and now.

As Joseph Pesch suggests, *The English Patient* conveys an apocalyptic sense of the end of history and civilization. This is established at several levels: through the breakdown of individuals, the English patient, Hana—"She was in rough shape herself... Partial shell shock probably." (p. 28)—and Caravaggio—"He was in near ruins." (p. 27); through the depiction of a landscape that is in ruins or about to explode or catch fire; and through the recurrent motif of the end of the world—"... [Caravaggio] was flung upwards and then down as part of the end of the world.... He swam up to the surface, parts of which were on fire" (p. 60); "*One day after we heard the bombs were dropped in Japan. So it feels like the end of the world*" (p. 292, italics in original).

With the sense of historical progress and civilization at an end, the characters, as Joseph Pesch suggests, are shown returning to the past in an attempt to stabilize their lives. In the case of Hana, the narrative returns to her childhood in Toronto, as the idealistic young girl who identifies with Verdi and sings the Marseillaise. It shows the gradual desensitization and breakdown caused by her continuous proximity to the dying and by the news of her father's death, and her decision to nurse the dying patient, a surrogate father, in an act of personal redemption. We are also given Caravaggio's past in Toronto, whose brilliance as thief and womanizer enables him to defy social control. The narrative shows him returning to the scenes of his torture by the Gestapo, the "time of darkness" (p. 61) this causes for him, and his attempt to motivate himself by saving Hana. The progressive revelation of Hana's and Caravaggio's pasts comes in a fragmented, non-sequential form; it introduces characters—Patrick, Hana's father, Clara her stepmother, Caravaggio's wife Gianetta—and elements of plot from Ondaatje's earlier novel, *In the Skin of A Lion*. Since these are not fully developed in *The English Patient*, there is a sense of the plot escaping its frame, going beyond its formal beginning by entangling itself in the narrative of another text. The ending of the novel also avoids formal closure by introducing the fictional author as narrator, speculating about possible futures for Kip and Hana: "And Hana moves possibly in the company that is not her choice . . . She is a woman I don't know well enough to hold in my wing, if writers have wings . . ." (p. 301).

Conventional linear development of plot is rejected in the treatment of the Almásy-Katharine relationship, which also illustrates the novel's complex use of narrative point of view and focalization. Their affair is narrated twice, firstly by third person narrator and secondly by Almásy himself. The effect of this is to disrupt chronological progression by contributing a sense of circularity to events. Temporal dislocation is enhanced by the use of a drugged narrator: "He rides the boat of morphine. It races in him, imploding time and geography the way maps compress the world onto a two-dimensional sheet of paper" (p. 161). In the third person narrative of the affair, the focalizer (the person from whose point of view the situation is experienced) shifts between Almásy, Katharine and an external observer. While in this version, Katharine's perspective is sometimes given, the second is exclusively from the egocentric perspective of Almásy. The strategy has the effect of questioning the objective, factual status of events, and suggests that these are subject to different valuations by different observers. Like Hana and Caravaggio, the English patient's long retrospective passages are partly an attempt to probe the past for some insight into the apocalyptic situation he finds himself in (p. 233).

In his attempt to "unthread the story out of [Almásy]," Caravaggio has a practical purpose, to establish the facts that will prove the English patient to have been the spy who worked for Rommel. This phase of the novel has elements of the espionage plot, as the details of Almásy's desert crossing with the German agent Kepler are uncovered. Such conventional plotting, however, undergoes what Igor Maver terms "a psychological decomposition," as, with the influence of morphine, the patient's factual narrative shifts into magical mode and he becomes the God Wepwawet, the jackal "with one eye that looks back and one that regards the path you consider taking. In his jaws are pieces of the past he delivers to you . . ." (p. 259). The description of Katharine's death gaze is followed by Almásy/Wepwawet's description of her first meeting with Clifton in the Oxford Union, so that past and present seem to share the same instant. This narrative technique confounds the reader's expectation of conventional linear sequence, as does Ondaatje's use of anticipation and repetition to link past and future events—like Kip catching the fuze box dropped by Caravaggio (p. 208) and the knife dropped by his daughter (p. 302).

Traditional forms of narration such as the use of the third person, anonymous, omniscient narrator suggest that reality is being represented from a stable center. The reader is reassured to find a consistent voice and perspective in the narrator. Postmodernist narrative forms, however, such as historiographic metafiction are characterized by the subversion of consistent point of view. Point of view and focalization are constantly shifting in *The English Patient*. Narration is flexible, moving between external focalizer and different character focalizers, between past and present, between first and third person, between different narrative modes, monologue, dialogue, the reading and writing of diary entries, literary, historical and documentary extracts. At times, narrative shifts are rapid and abrupt in a manner that undermines the reader's sense of a stable center of consciousness. It is particularly in relation to the English patient that concepts of the unified subject are questioned. From the opening description of him "dragging the listening heart of the young nurse beside him to wherever his mind is, into that well of memory he kept plunging into during those months before he died" (p. 4), the novel suggests a precarious subjectivity that ranges across fragments of the past: "He speaks in fragments of oasis towns, the later Medicis, the prose style of Kipling, the woman who bit into his flesh. And in his commonplace book . . . are fragments . . . All that is missing is his own name" (p. 7). As Caravaggio becomes more intent on establishing his identity, the English patient's narration shifts from first to third person, confounding the reader's assumption of a stable ego: "There are days when I come home from arid writing . . . Almásy was drunk and attempting an old dance step he had invented called the Bosphorus hug . . . *Who is he speaking as now?* Caravaggio thinks" (pp. 243–4). "Who was talking back there? *Death means you are in the third person*" (p. 247).

Ondaatje's approach to narrative form in *The English Patient* shows the influence of his poetry. From the novel's opening, the development of plot and character is informed by a pattern of image and symbol. As Ondaatje has explained, the initial imaginative impulse for the novel came from an image rather than theme, situation or character: "I usually begin books in a dreamlike — no, that sounds a little esoteric. But I had this little fragment of a guy who had crashed in the desert. I didn't know who he was, or anything" (Ondaatje, quoted by Scobie, *World and I*, p. 301). The opening chapter, "The Villa," treats Hana and the English patient as anonymous "she" and "he", which encourages symbolic associations to cluster rather than individuated character. The description, "I flew down and the sand itself caught fire . . . The leather helmet on my head in flames . . . It was the time of the war in heaven" (p. 5), with its allusion to Milton's *Paradise Lost*, suggests the fall of Satan from Heaven to Hell. Earlier, there is Hana's view of him as Christ, a "despairing saint," while the Bedouin who treats him is described as an archangel standing over "the supine body with his wings," as "the baptist" who anoints him with his oils. These images figure themes that appear later in the novel, the fall though pride, political ambition, the possibility of redemption through suffering, communal comfort.

Stephen Scobie has analyzed the structural role of fire in *The English Patient*. The opening image of the man falling in flames to the desert is repeated by the patient in a passage that draws attention to the paradox of beauty and destruction in fire: "Then his legs are free of everything, and he is in the air, bright, not knowing why he is bright until he realises he is on fire" (p. 175). The motif is taken up in relation to Caravaggio's escape from the Gestapo (p. 60), Kip's bomb disposal work (pp. 105, 211, 213) and after the German evacuation of Naples there is a possibility that "the city would dissolve in flames" (p. 276). These references to fire prepare for the novel's climax and the news of nuclear bombs on Hiroshima and Nagasaki, "like a burst map, the hurricane of heat withering bodies as it meets them . . ." (p. 284). The motif of fire and explosion is clearly linked to the novel's apocalyptic theme (p. 60), and evokes a landscape of desolation caused by Western civilization's obsession with power. However, as has been seen, *The English Patient* draws on mythic patterns of sterility and death followed by renewal and life, and the prevalence of fire in the novel is counterbalanced by frequent references to water. The motif of fire connects the political with the personal. Hana reads from the English patient's diary: "The heart is an organ of fire . . . A love story is . . . a consuming of oneself and the past" (p. 97), subtly linking the paradox of destruction and creation in its personal and public dimensions as when the flames from Kip's flare light up the splendor of the frescoes in the Italian church.

THE PROBLEM OF POLITICS IN *THE ENGLISH PATIENT*

Linda Hutcheon, Ajay Heble and Geetha Ganapathy-Dore have positioned Ondaatje's work within a postcolonial context, as a protest on behalf of the marginalized, ex-centric subject against the economic and cultural dominance of a patriarchal, Imperial West. A number of American critics, however, have been critical of the book's politics — Craig Seligman in *The New Republic*, Hilary Mantel in *The New York Review of Books*, Morton Kaplan and Michael Marshall in a special edition devoted to the novel in *The World and I* (a review with close links to *The Washington Times*). Marshall cites two comments on the novel by Ondaatje — "I wanted all the uniforms removed," "Right from the start I was aware that it was a very political book" — and concludes "The tension between these comments leaves the book seriously flawed."

Criticism has focused on the ending of the novel, the dropping of the atomic bombs and Kip's abrupt conversion from Anglophile to Anti-Western Sikh nationalist. Stephen Scobie has shown how the climax of the nuclear holocaust has been prepared for through the accumulation of images and incidents relating to fire, and Nicholas Spice sees the news of Hiroshima and Nagasaki as a "skilful mechanism for ending the novel," representing a moment of truth that demsytifies Kip about the Western values he has assimilated. For most critics, however, Kip's anti-Western outburst on hearing the news of the bombs on his shortwave radio is an artistic flaw — a crude polemic that is out of key with the subtle psychological developments that have been taking place amongst the group in the villa. At the technical level, it has been suggested that Ondaatje is guilty of anachronism in giving Kip a post-1960's consciousness of the impact of a nuclear bomb on a city, which would have been unimaginable for him in 1945 (but is this necessarily the case?).

According to these critics, Kip's sudden change of allegiance confirms a weakness of characterization in Ondaatje's work. As the most complex of the novel's characters in his negotiation of a double heritage, Kip is "let down" by the author who turns him into an abstraction, Asia, and makes him a mouthpiece for Ondaatje's own outbursts against the iniquity of Empire. Futhermore, in a novel that proclaims nationality as the enemy and offers a model community in the villa that has transcended racial boundaries, there is a serious contradiction in the spectacle of Kip directing racially based generalizations against the West in a way that does not seem to carry any implied qualification. Seligman goes so far as to suggest that these tensions stem from Ondaatje's own conflicting loyalties and conflicted sense of identity as a migrant from Asia to North America: "At the end of the novel, Ondaatje who has been accused of disloyalty to his Third World origins . . . proudly allies himself with the Asians . . . But you have only to read him to realise that whatever his racial mix, he is as Western as Billy the Kid." Kip's identification of Japan with "Asia", as a victim of Western oppression, has also raised problems, in view of Japan's own history of imperial expansion and atrocities against China and the Asian subcontinent. However, since this is a point which Kip himself had made about Japan against his own anti-imperialist brother, it is possible to see his invocation of "Asia" as ironized in the context of the novel as a whole. Ondaatje's harshest reviewers, Morton Kaplan and Michael Marshall, have criticized the fact that Kip's statement "They would never have dropped an atom bomb on a white nation" is allowed to stand unchallenged and unexamined through a more rigorous historical assessment of the situation at the end of the Second World War. Seligman and Marshall also take issue with the political philosophy expressed in Hana's statement after the atom bombs on Japanese cities and Kip's departure: "From now on I believe the personal will be forever at war with the public" (p. 292).

Similar to the statement made by Hana's stepfather in *In the Skin of A Lion*, "The trouble with ideology, Alice, is that it hates the private. You must make it human" (p. 135), it seems to represent a position that is at least partially endorsed in the two novels. In plot terms, the higher claim of the private over the public is shown in Almásy's readiness to betray the allies in order to obtain transport from the Germans to recover Katharine's body, and in Caravaggio's final acknowledgement that it did not matter which side the patient was on during the war. However, these critics argue that it is not possible to separate the private from the public, that the values the group in the villa were trying to salvage would not have survived in a totalitarian fascist world. Marshall argues that by underplaying the extent of Nazi atrocities (except for the scene of Caravaggio's torture), the novel fails to recognize that a German victory would have established a world order involving persecution of Jews, homosexuals, gypsies.

Critics have also found problems with Kip's final act, in which he abandons the set of relationships which have formed a new family for him at the villa. The reader has witnessed the gradual establishment of intimacy through shared affinities crossing cultures, generations, races. Kip's readiness to abandon his friends and loved ones for the sake of some poorly defined concept of national and ethnic loyalty has therefore been seen as the act of a moral adolescent. It also seems to conflict with the novel's advocacy of the private as exercising a higher claim and, even more fundamentally, with its profound scepticism about nationalistic allegiances.

The ending of the novel has thus raised a number of contentious issues. It is possible that more space needed to be given to the issue of the atomic bombing of Japanese cities and to Kip's motivation after his rejection of the West in order to allow his characterization to retain the psychological depth created in the earlier part of the novel. This may have made *The English Patient* a more political work than Ondaatje intended, but in the light of his own comment that "it is a very political work," the important political issues perhaps needed to be more carefully worked through. There is an element of irony in Kaplan's defence of the atomic bombs on Hiroshima and Nagasaki, which is, of course, the official Western account. Ondaatje's fiction is driven by the need to contest precisely such dominant versions of the past. Kip's assertion of a Sikh racial identity and a nationalist politics at the end of the novel seems at first sight to run counter to the novel's earlier rejection of nations and racial identity and its celebration of cultural hybridity. As such it would seem to represent inconsistency and contradiction, more serious artistic and intellectual flaws. The apparent inconsistencies can be understood in relation to the strategies that Ondaatje had developed in his earlier work *Running in the Family* for coming to terms with the migrant's "double perspective." As Ajay Heble has argued, the earlier work shows a tension between Ondaatje's celebration of cultural syncretism on the one hand and his desire to recover and assert pre-colonial values. A similar tension drives *The English Patient*. On the one hand, there is the privileging of the marginalized, the hybrid, the "international bastards," which finds its formal counterpart in postmodernist strategies that undermine fixed cognitive structures and the notion of the centered subject. On the other hand, the novel expresses a sympathy for anti-British nationalist projects such as those of Kip's brother and later Kip. It also shows a nostalgia for presence, for narratives of origin and essentialist modes of conceiving selfhood: "She holds an Indian goddess in her arms. She holds wheat and ribbons" (p. 218). "At this table all their hands are brown. They move with ease in their customs and habits" (p. 301). In its attempt to represent the exile's sense of displacement and hybridity, and also to enter into the indigenous third world subject's experience of anti-colonial resistance and ethnicity, Ondaatje is engaged in an imaginative attempt to resolve problems of the migrant's double perspective.

3

The Novel's Reception

 The English Patient is Ondaatje's most successful work to date. It was winner of Canada's Governor-General's Prize, winner of the Trillium Award, co-winner of the Booker Prize in 1992. The film version of 1997 won an Oscar for its director, Anthony Minghella, and the Picador paperback edition alone has sold three quarters of a million copies. Reviewers recognized the brilliance and imaginative scope of the novel. Judith Grossman, in *The New York Times Book Review*, found it "an intensely theatrical tour de force, but grounded in Michael Ondaatje's strong feeling for distant times and places," while Pico Iyer in *Time* wrote that "Out of these ghostly materials, Michael Ondaatje has fashioned a magic carpet of a novel that soars across worlds and times." In view of its success, it is surprising that *The English Patient* has drawn a significant amount of adverse criticism, and generated widely divergent judgements of some of its most distinctive features. This suggests considerable variation in the terms on which the novel has been assessed. As has been seen, the novel is particularly resistant to easy classification of its form and genre.

Most reviewers have commented on its language, usually felt to have been influenced by Ondaatje's first career as a poet. Linda Hutcheon suggested in *The Nation* that, but for "the lapidary quality of its language and its almost formal architecture of rhythm and mood," *The English Patient* could have been seen as a Canadian *Farewell to Arms*. Whitney Balliett found "passages of such finesse and vividness [in the novel] that they become part of us," and suggested that "At its most compressed [as in the description of the desert storm], Ondaatje's writing strikingly recalls the last of the great French aphorists and pensée writers, Jules Renard." Others have found the language too brilliant and showy, "overprecious, stylistic cleverness" (Tom Clarke in *The World and I*). Nicholas Spice, in *The London Review of Books*, submitted a number of Ondaatje's more striking images to detailed analysis and concluded that these images were unsuccessful, since "for figurative language to succeed it must work at the level of ordinary meaning as well as allusion." But this seems based on a misconception of Ondaatje's poetic practice which has always succeeded most when it works the fine line between formal control and a freer volatile creativity. Spice also ignores the role of specific figures within the novel's wider symbolic and thematic structure and in establishing an emotional color and disinctive narrative voice — with a savant's breadth of knowledge and an aesthete's appreciation of cadence and sensuous richness. In fact, a number of critics found themselves overwhelmed with the sheer beauty of Ondaatje's language, its "enamelled, butterfly sheen" (Sage), "shimmering with the brilliance of Arab poetry" (Iyer). So much so that Craig Seligman in *The New Republic* expressed surprise at "the exquisite restraint of the language" given the violence of the subject matter, particulary since "as a poet, Ondaatje specializes in the shocking image, the exhilirating grotesquerie."

The novel's narrative structure has also drawn some significantly different responses. For Whitney Balliett in *The New Yorker* and Hilary Mantel in *The New York Review of Books*, the novel failed to develop strong, coherent plots. Mantel felt the absence of a strong narrative core able to sustain the novel: "To create a still center, to let the narrative ripple around it: this is a useful, graceful technique. Strangely it is here that grace fails. Ondaatje's narrative becomes uneven, unresolved, unsatisfactory. It is . . . as if the power that should belong in the story had drained away." Such criticism suggests a reader expecting the all-absorbing plot of a traditional realist novel. By contrast, Lorna Sage in *The Times Literary Supplement* admired Ondaatje's technical virtuosity: "Michael Ondaatje's special gift as a novelist is to keep all the elements of a story in suspension, up in the air, seeming still yet buzzing with life, like a juggler's dinner service." Describing Ondaatje as a bricoleur, a handyman joining together narrative fragments, Sage subscribes to a more contemporary fictional model, like Tom Clarke who sees the novel as a postmodernist narrative with a complex "layering of structural figures," and deliberate disruption of linear sequence. Generally, critics have felt the strongest storylines to be those relating to Kip and the desert explorations, the weakest the fatal love affair between Katharine and Almásy.

A number of critics recognized that the novel's narrative unity rests not on linear plotting but the repetition of key structural figures and images. Stephen Scobie's important study on the role of fire has been referred to in the section above on the novel, and Beverley Slopen writing in the *Publisher's Weekly* quoted Ondaatje himself on the influence of visual art forms on his approach to narrative structure: "a story can be knit together by images. This seems to me a less didactic method of building a theme." When reviewers moved away from considerations of "storyline," they recognized a formal unity in the structure of *The English Patient*, which Barbara Leckie in *The Canadian Forum* found "finely wrought and carefully balanced."

Ondaatje's critics have had problems with another element of the traditional novel, characterization. Seligman asks, "Are the characters supposed to represent individuals, or are they abstractions?" and feels that the tension between the two "pulls at the narrative again and again, [and] finally ends up ripping it down the middle." He finds the motivation of the characters simplified (Hana caring for the patient because her own father had been burned), and revealing a love of "big theatrical behaviour," as when Kip walks out on the group in the villa. Mantel finds "Hana and Kip under-realized, [while] the sapper is idealized," concluding that Ondaatje's characters are "wraiths freighted with abstraction, weighed down with portent." Bill Fledderus answers these charges by pointing to the element of myth and romance in the novel. "But to take Ondaatje's novel on its own terms requires accounting for its allegiance to Arthurian romance and myth. And in many cases characters are secondary to structure in romance." Characters in myth and romance may not be significant in terms of psychological complexity and consistency, but as exemplifications of ritual patterns and mythic themes. And yet, as Fledderus recognizes, there is sufficient historical detail in *The English Patient* to make it understandable that critics should approach it as a realist text. This suggests that the novel's crossing of genre boundaries has sometimes made it difficult for critics to establish the terms on which to judge *The English Patient*.

Of those reviewers attempting to define the novel's themes, most agreed that its central preoccupation was with displacement and the figure of the outsider, particularly with those finding themselves in a complex and problematic relationship with a declining British Empire (Hutcheon; Slopen; and Sage). Slopen quoted Ondaatje's own statement of concern "for all those people born in one place who live in another place, who have lost their source." It is the politics of the novel, however, which have generated the most extreme and divergent responses from critics, and this aspect of the critical response has been addressed in depth in the section on the novel itself. There has been a considerable amount written on Ondaatje, his earlier works and on *The English Patient*. Some of the most useful have been referred to in the sections above and a select bibliography can be found below. The following websites also contain some interesting material:

www.barclayagency.com/ondaatje.html

www.cariboo.bc.ca/ae/engml/FRIEDMAN/ondaatje.html

www.powells.com/authors/ondaatje961118.html

www.salonmagazine.com/nov96/ondaatje961118.html

4

The Novel on Film

The film version of *The English Patient* appeared in 1996
to as great an acclaim as the novel, winning nine Academy awards,
including Best Picture, Best Director for Anthony Minghella, Best
Supporting Actress for Juliette Binoche as Hana. Ondaatje collaborated on the film, and commented,

What we have now are two stories, one with the pace and detail of a three
hundred page novel and one that is the length of a vivid and subtle film.
Each has its own organic structure. There are obvious differences and
values, but somehow each version deepens the other and what is most
interesting to me about the film is how scenes and emotions and values
from the book emerged in new ways, were re-invented, were invented with
totally new moments, and fit within a dramatic arc that was different from
the book. (Ondaatje, quoted by Stenberg, *Literature/Film Quartely*, p. 255).

Ondaatje felt that though the two versions had a different dramatic mo-
mentum and structure appropriate to each medium, they nevertheless
complement one another in a deeper sense. Reviewers of the film such
as Raymond Aaron Younis and Jacqui Sadashige have not been so
sure. Minghella's comment on the film is surely significant here,

[*The English Patient*] is above all a romantic film . . . Almásy and Katharine, the central protagonists . . . feel a fatal inevitability to their love. It's as
if an irresistible force is bringing them together and they're helpless in the
face of their destiny. And their destiny is affected by everything around
them. (*The English Patient* Press Kit. Miramax Films.)

The multiple story lines of the book are narrowed down so that the
film can concentrate on the fatal love affair between Almásy and
Katharine, which Younis suggests has been recast in keeping with
the conventions of a love story with melodramatic elements. The
relative importance of Hana and Katharine has been reversed. The
aeroplane flight with Katharine's dead body opens and closes
the film. Her character is developed more, as the intelligent upperclass beauty exploring new areas of experience while retaining a
nostalgia for her English roots. Some sharp dialogue has been introduced to trace the gradual revelation of powerful suppressed desire.
In keeping with the conventions of love melodrama, the Katharine-
Almásy relationship in the film is seen in terms of a conflict between love and duty. This is most clearly seen in the added episode
where the frenzied passion of the adulterous couple is glimpsed
through a patriotic Christmas party for British soldiers. Melodrama
indeed. The staples of such a genre — desire vs. duty, irrationality vs.
convention — are milked in such scenes, as, later, is the figure of the
jealous husband who follows Katharine's taxi to Almásy's rooms. (In
the novel, Geoffrey Clifton is shown to be unaware of his wife's
betrayal until his final attempt to kill them all with the aeroplane).
Two incidents will show how the novel's wider themes are subordi-
nated to the love interest. In the film, Almásy's review of different
winds is delivered to Katharine not Hana, and signals their first
moment of easy intimacy. In the book his descriptions have a quite
different role — to establish the theme of geographical diversity and
the ethnographic range of Almásy's own knowledge as the interna-

tionalist. The one use of Herodotus in the film is Katharine's re-counting of the Gyges-Candaules episode. Herodotus is thus used to mark a moment of pyscho-sexual crisis in the Almásy-Katharine-Geoffrey love triangle, as Minghella's screenplay makes clear, and the significance of Herodotus in the novel's more philosophic inter-est in the interaction of ancient and contemporary narratives is barely alluded to. The desert itself—in the book a metaphor for the shifting grounds and transience of territorial possession—is in the film eroticised as a sensual human body in some memorable aerial photography. The desert thus forms an exquisite frame, as prelude and epilogue to a love story.

In its concentration on the love triangle, other characters are changed or simplified. The film reduces Hana's motives in caring for the patient to a matter of her duty as a nurse. Her motives in the book have greater complexity and resonance—as consecration of herself for her dead father and as a mythic quest for redemption in a world bereft of value. The figure of Kip is also simplified. His complex subjectivity as Sikh, sapper, Anglophile and anti-colonial is barely hinted at, as he assumes the role of Hana's lover, and the film is more concerned with the balance achieved in his relation-ship with Hana and the counterpoint this offers with the all-consuming passion of Katharine and Almásy. The film makes no reference to the atom bombs on Hiroshima and Nagasaki. Conse-quently, Kip's political awakening and assertion of Asian national-ism is elided. The motivation at his break with Hana and the group in the villa is instead provided by the death of his subordinate Hardy. Kip is made to recognize the failure of personal communi-cation between himself and his loyal English NCO despite their mutual love and respect and sharing of many dangers. The film here offers a sentimental restatement of the theme of love crossed by social barriers and idealises the British-Asian relationship in a way that runs quite counter to the ending of the novel.

Stenberg argues that the significance of the patient himself is transformed in the film. In the book, the anonymity of the patient, the absence of facial expression, figures the elusiveness of identity, and the patient himself is seen differently by different viewers — saint, spy, lover, explorer. . . . Minghella's screenplay makes it the film's business to fix the patient's identity. The patient's face is made expressive of a range of feelings and a distinct personality and character. Caravaggio's interrogations are given an added urgency by the motive of personal revenge, and the flashbacks create a coherent story of a passion destroyed in its attempt to transcend social barriers. At the end of the film, the patient persuades Hana to give him an overdose of morphine. He dies listening to Katharine's last words in the cave and the visual sequence of their final flight is repeated as his last moment of consciousness. The film's patient does not evade definition but achieves "closure" as the tragic romantic lover.

A number of the novel's themes and motifs are sketched in within the tighter frame of the film: the idea of mapping as analogue for ownership, of territory and people; the way in which the internationalism of the desert explorers is overtaken by nationalistic rivalries and suspicions at the onset of war; Kip has one anti-imperial speech while reading Kipling's *Kim* to the patient. But these appear as the merest traces of issues explored in much greater depth in the book. The film also does give some sense of the novel's structure and form through the use of rapid cutting between past and present, and it also tries to suggest the book's fluid shifts between narrators, for example, when the Gyges-Candaules episode is shared between Katharine and Hana as narrators. The film's focus on the strong plot line of the love story, however, stabilizes the narrative in a way that is quite different from the novel's postmodernist manipulation of multiple plot lines, intertextuality, and its decomposition of plot and point of view as it moves to its climax.

5

Further Reading and Discussion Questions

In his last two works since *The English Patient*, the novel *Anil's Ghost* (2000) and *Handwriting* (1998), Ondaatje returns to the country of his birth. The setting of *Anil's Ghost* is closely based on the grim reality of Sri Lanka in the early 1990s, a country traumatized by civil war between the government, the insurgents in the South and the Tamil separatists in the North. The heroine, Anil Tissera, a Sri Lankan who has been educated in England and the United States, is chosen to represent the United Nations in an investigation of human rights abuses in Sri Lanka. Paired with a Sri Lankan archaeologist, she discovers, amongst the ancient remains of a government archaeological site, a skeleton that is clearly of recent date, and the evidence points to an extra-judicial killing. It is the quest to reconstitute "Sailor"—his appearance, manner and place of work, the location and form of his execution—that becomes the central metaphor of the novel, representing the possibility that the marginalized subject might yet outface the attempt by the powerful to elide his presence from the official account. The novel's concern with archaeology and forensic pathology takes *Anil's Ghost* into territory familiar from *The English Patient*, the status of historical truth. Anil, herself, described as "the prodigal returned," is another of the exile figures familiar from Ondaatje's earlier writings and interviews. The novel presents her in broken personal relationships and torn between a desire for the freedom of the exile and a nostalgia for her Sri Lankan childhood, whose rich textures are evoked with Ondaatje's characteristic vividness. Formally, the novel recalls the structure of his earlier works: a central plot based on the detection or revelation of an enigmatic individual is interspersed with documentary style passages—on Sri Lankan geography, natural history, treatises on the treatment of war injuries, the system of mining gems—and quick cutting between the central characters' present experiences and fragments of past relationships. *Handwriting* (1998) is a collection of poems written in Sri Lanka and Canada between 1993 and 1998. Like *Anil's Ghost*, it points up the contradictions of Sri Lanka, juxtaposing contemporary scenes of political violence with the island's traditions of Buddhist and Hindu piety and civilized codes of behavior, the remnants of which are still traceable in the remains of ancient forest sanctuaries. Its title points to the faith it shares with *Anil's Ghost* in the persistence of the human record, whatever forms this may take and whatever the means used by the powerful to suppress it.

QUESTIONS FOR DISCUSSION

1. Ondaatje has said in an interview that the novel is about a process of healing. What is the nature of that process for each of the characters who gather in the Villa San Girolamo?

2. Almásy announces that he hates ownership and naming. How is this point of view explored and assessed through the public and private plots of the novel?

3. Ondaatje has emphasized the central importance of Kip's relationship with the English patient. Examine the relationship closely giving reasons for the author's view.

4. Herodotus is referred to in the novel as the father of history and the father of lies. In what ways does the novel problematize the relationship between historical fact and fiction?

5. "Kip and I are international bastards." How is the position of the exile explored and evaluated particularly in the light of the novel's ending?

6. Assess the novel's treatment of political themes. Do Ondaatje's comments, "I wanted all the uniforms removed," "Right from the start I was aware that it was a very political book," point to a confusion in the novel's treatment of political issues? Consider in particular the ending of the novel, Kip's response to the atomic bombing of Hiroshima and Nagasaki.

7. In his interviews, Ondaatje has revealed the care he has taken to research and establish the setting of his novel. Consider the novel's treatment of different physical environments and cultural locations. Are these merely "background" or do they contribute substantially to the central issues being explored in the novel?

8. Discuss the novel's treatment of gender in the light of the following comments by critics "So you could say that the theme of *The English Patient* is . . . the death of the patriarchal scarecrow" (Lorna Sage). "Thus the male narrative of desert exploration, of self-sufficiency gives way to a male version of the love story" (Paul Hjartarson).

9. How successful do you find the narrative structure and use of point of view in the novel? In what ways do these formal features contribute to the development of wider thematic issues?

10. Reviewers have suggested that *The English Patient* shows the influence of Ondaatje's poetry. Consider how symbols and images are used to structure the novel and develop its main themes.

11. *The English Patient* has been described as an example of "the Research Novel" because of the meticulous research that went into the novel's treatment of areas of professional knowledge. Ondaatje himself has said in an interview, "As a writer, I find certain professions fascinating." Consider some examples of the novel's use of "technical literature" suggesting what the function of such material might be.

12. In his review of the novel, Craig Seligman comments that "Ondaatje goes after his subject with his poet's flair for startling images. But what rings like a bell within the confines of a poem may not carry so far in the wide-open landscape of the novel." Collect some examples of highly figurative language, similes and metaphors, and argue a case for or against their use in the contexts in which they appear.

13. The English patient's story is cradled in the margins of Herodotus's *Histories*, and this is paradigmatic of the novel's dependence on earlier narratives, myths, works of art. Consider the relationship between the plots and characters of the novel and some of the earlier myths, narratives and images to which they are related. How successful do you find the use of 'intertextuality' in the novel?

14. It would be a rewarding exercise to compare *The English Patient* to other works, and the following are suggestions that might be considered.
    I. An obvious point to begin would be to compare *The English Patient* with Ondaatje's own fiction. The works that offer particularly productive grounds of comparison in

terms of form and theme are probably *In the Skin of A Lion* (1987), an extremely rich and interesting work, and his latest novel, set in Sri Lanka, *Anil's Ghost* (2000). The work of another Sri Lankan immigrant to Canada, Shyam Selvadurai's *Funny Boy* (1995), would be interesting to look at as an insight into the social and cultural context of Ceylon, which it links to the problems of identity being experienced by a young boy coming to terms with his sexuality.

II. Margaret Atwood's *Surfacing* (1992) would be useful to consider, since it is a work that explores the problem of Canadian national identity and relates this to issues of gender, thus providing a useful insight into the Canadian literary milieu in which Ondaatje emerged as a writer.

III. It would also be valuable to compare the novel with works by writers who have undergone the same experience of migration and write from a similar position of ex-centricity: Salman Rushdie's *Midnight's Children* (1981), Kazuo Ishiguro's *The Remains of the Day* (1989), and works by Timothy Mo, such as *Soursweet* (1992).

IV. These writers engage with issues of national identity and cultural hybridity which are also central concerns of *The English Patient*, and it would be interesting to consider works that consider these themes in very different settings or genres, Brian Friel's *Translations* (1981), Aladair Gray's *Lanark* (1991), and Carlos Fuentes' *The Old Gringo* (1987).

V. Finally, it would be interesting to compare the novel with novels from an earlier period dealing with similar situations or themes: Ernest Hemingway's *Farewell to Arms* (1929), or novels of Empire such as E. M. Forster's *Passage to India* (1924), Kipling's *Kim* (1901), Paul Scott's *Jewel In the Crown* (1966).

BIBLIOGRAPHY

Selected Works by Michael Ondaatje

Longer Works:

The Collected Works of Billy the Kid: Left Handed Poems. Toronto: Anansi, 1970. London: Macmillan/Picador, 1989.

Coming Through Slaughter. Toronto: Anansi, 1976. London: Macmillan/ Picador, 1984.

Running in the Family. Toronto: McClelland and Stewart, 1982. London: Mamillan/Picador, 1984.

In the Skin of A Lion. New York: Alfred A. Knopf, 1987; Toronto: Mc-Clelland and Stewart, 1987. London: Picador, 1987.

The English Patient. New York: Alfred A. Knopf, 1992; Toronto: Mc-Clelland and Stewart, 1992; London: Bloomsbury, 1992.

Anil's Ghost. New York: Alfred A. Knopf, 2000; Toronto: McLelland and Stewart, 2000; London: Bloomsbury, 2000.

Poetry

The Dainty Monsters. Toronto: Coach House Press, 1967.

The man with seven toes. Toronto. Coach House Press, 1969.

Rat Jelly. Toronto: Coach House, 1973.

There's A Trick with a Knife I'm Learning to Do: Poems 1963–1978. New York: Norton, 1979; Toronto: McClelland and Stewart, 1979.

Rat Jelly and Other Poems: 1963–78. London: Marion Boyars, 1980.

Elimination Dance. Ilderton, Ontario: Nairn, 1978.

Tin Roof. Lantzville, B.C.: Island, 1982.

Secular Love. Toronto: Coach House Press, 1984.

The Cinammon Peeler: Selected Poems. London: Pan Books, 1989; New York: Alfred A. Knopf, 1991; Toronto: McClelland and Stewart, 1992

Handwriting. New York: Alfred A. Knopf, 1998; Toronto: McClelland and Stewart, 1998; London: Bloomsbury, 1998.

Critical Study

Leonard Cohen. Canadian Writers Series 5. Toronto: McClelland, 1970.

Films and Screenplays

Sons of Captain Poetry. Mongrel Films/Canadian Film-Makers Distribution Centre, 1970 (Director).

The Clinton Special. Mongrel Films/Canadian Film-Makers Distribution Centre, 1972 (producer and director).

Select Criticism

Works on Cultural Context

Berger, Carl. *The Writing of Canadian History: Aspects of English-Canadian Historical Writing since 1900*. 2nd ed. Toronto: University of Toronto Press, 1986.

Bhabha, Homi. *The Location of Culture*. London, New York: Routledge, 1994.

Cavell, Richard. "Where is Frye? Or, Theorizing Postcolonial Space." *Esssays in Canadian Writing* 56 (Fall 1995), 110–135.

Foucault, Michel. and Rabinow, Paul, eds. *The Foucault Reader. An Introduction to Foucault's Thought*. London, NewYork, Toronto: Penguin, 1991.

Frye, Northrop. *The Bush Garden, Essays on the Canadian Imagination*. Toronto: Anansi, 1971.

Hall, Stuart. "Ethnicity: Identity and Difference." *Radical America* 23.4 (1991), 9–20.

Howells, Coral Ann, and Hunter, Lynette eds. *Narrative Strategies in Canadian Literature: Feminism and Postcolonialism*. Buckingham: Open University Press, 1991.

Huggan, Graham. "Decolonizing the Map." Bill Ashcroft, Gareth Griffiths, Helen Tiffin eds., *The Post-Colonial Studies Reader*. London, New York: Routledge, 1995, 407–411.

Hutcheon Linda. *A Poetics of Postmodernism*. New York and London: Routledge, 1988.

———. *The Canadian Postmodern, A Study of Contemporary English-Canadian Fiction*. Toronto, New York, Oxford: Oxford University Press, 1988.

Jameson, Fredric. *Postmodernism or, The Cultural Logic of Late Capitalism*. New York and London: Verso, 1991.

Lawson, Alan. "Post-Colonial Theory and the 'Settler' Subject." *Esssays in Canadian Writing*. 56 (Fall 1995), 20–36.

Lyotard, François. *The Postmodern Condition: A Report on Knowledge*. Manchester: Manchester University Press, 1984.

Mandel, Eli, ed. *Contexts of Canadian Criticism*. Chicago, London: University of Chicago Press, 1971.

Said, Edward. *Orientalism*. London: Routledge, 1978.

Slemon, Stephen. "Unsettling the Empire: Resistance Theory for the Second World". *World Literature Written in English* 30.2 (1990), 30–41.

Works on or Connected with The English Patient

Balliett, Whitney. "*The English Patient*" (Book Review). *The New Yorker*, 68.42 (December 7 1992), 161–3.

Clarke, Tom. "On Foreign Ground". *The World and I*, (February 1993), 311–315.

Cook, Rufus. "Imploding Time and Geography: Narrative Compressions in Michael Ondaatje's *The English Patient*." *The Journal of Commonwealth Literature*, 33.2 (Fall 1998), 109–126.

Ellis, Susan. "Trade and Power, Money and War: Rethinking Masculinity in Michael Ondaatje's *The English Patient*." *Studies in Canadian Literature*, 21.2(1996), 22–36.

Ganapathy-Dore, Geetha. "The Novel of the Nowhere Man: Michael Ondaatje's *The English Patient*." *Commonwealth Essays and Studies*, 16.2 (1993), 96–100.

Grossman, Judith. "*The English Patient*" (Book Review). *The New York Times Book Review*, (November 1 1992), 7–10.

Hjartarson, Paul. "*The English Patient*" (Book Review). *Canadian Literature*, 142–3 (Fall-Winter 1994), 234–6.

Hutcheon, Linda. *"The English Patient"* (Book Review). *The Nation*, 256.1 (January 4 1993), 22–25.

Iyer, Pico. *"The English Patient"* (Book Review). *Time*, 140.18 (November 2), 71–3.

Kaplan, Morton and Marshall, Michael. Editorial (On *The English Patient*). *The World and I*, (February 1993).

Leckie, Barbara. *"The English Patient"* (Book Review). *The Canadian Forum*, 71.816 (January–February 1993), 39–42.

Lernout, Gert. "Michael Ondaatje: The Desert of the Soul." *Kunapipi*, 14.2 (1992), 124–6.

Mantel, Hilary. *"The English Patient"* (Book Review). *The New York Review of Books*, 40.1–2 (January 14 1993), 22–24.

Marshall, Michael. "The Politics of the *The English Patient*." *The World and I*, (February 1993), 316–320.

Minghella, Anthony. *The English Patient, A Screenplay*. London, Toronto: Methuen, 1997.

Pesch, Joseph. "Post-Apocalyptic War Histories: Michael Ondaatje's *The English Patient*." *Ariel*, 28.2 (April 1997). 117–140.

Roxburgh, David. "The gospel of Almásy: Christian mythology in Michael Ondaatje's *The English Patient*." *Essays on Canadian Writing*, 1.67 (Spring 1999), 236–254.

Sadashige, Jacqui. "Sweeping the Sands of Desire in *The English Patient*." *Literature/Film Quarterly*, 26.4 (1998), 242–254.

Sage, Lorna. *"The English Patient"* (Book Review). *The Times Literary Supplement*, 4667 (September 11, 1992), 23–4.

Scobie, Stephen. "The Reading Lesson: Michael Ondaatje and the Patients of Desire." *Essays on Canadian Writing*. (Michael Ondaatje Issue), 53 (Summer 1994), 92–107.

———. "The Heart is an Organ of Fire," *The World and I*, (February 1993), 301–310.

Seligman, Craig. *"The English Patient"* (Book Review). *The New Republic*, 208.11 (March 15 1993).

Simpson, Mark. D. "Minefield Readings: The Postcolonial English Patient." *Essays on Canadian Writing*. (Michael Ondaatje Issue), 53 (Summer 1994), 216–237.

Slopen, Beverley. "Michael Ondaatje: transplanted from Ceylon to Canada, he writes about 'people born in one place who live in another place.'" *Publishers Weekly*, 239.44 (October 5 1992), 48–50.

Spice, Nicholas. "Ways of being a Man. *The English Patient* by Michael Ondaatje," *London Review of Books*, 14 (September 24, 1992), 3.

Stenberg, Douglas G. "A Firmament in the Midst of the Waters: Dimensions of Love in *The English Patient*." *Literature/Film Quarterly*, 26.4 (1998), 255–262.

Thorpe, Michael. *"The English Patient"* (Book Review). *World Literature Today*, 67.3 (Summer 1993), 608–12.

Williams, David. "The Politics of Cyborg Communication: Harold Innis, Marshall McLuhan and *The English Patient*," *Canadian Literature*, 156 (Spring 1998), 30–55.

Younis, Raymond Aaron. "Nationhood and Decolonization in *The English Patient*." *Literature-Film Quarterly*, 26.1 (January 1998), 2–10.

de Zepetnek, Stephen Tostoy. *"The English Patient:* 'Truth is Stranger than Fiction.'" *Essays on Canadian Writing*, (Michael Ondaatje Issue) 53 (Summer 1994), 141–153.

On Michael Ondaatje and his other works

Barbour, Douglas. *Michael Ondaatje*. Twayne's World Authors Series: Canadian Literature, 835. New York: Twayne-Macmillan, 1993.

Beran, Carol L. "Ex-Centricity: Michael Ondaatje's *In the Skin of A Lion* and Hugh McLennan's Barometer Rising." *Studies in Canadian Literature*, 18.1 (1993), 71–84.

Bok, Christian. "Destructive Creation: the Politicization of Violence in the Works of Michael Ondaatje."*Canadian Literature*, 132(Spring 1992), 109–124.

Bush, Catherine. "Michael Ondaatje: an Interview." *Essays on Canadian Writing*, (Michael Ondaatje Issue) 53 (Summer 1994), 238–249.

Clarke, George Eliot. "Michael Ondaatje and the Production of Myth". *Studies in Canadian Literature 16.1*, (1991), 1–21.

Dabydeen, Cyril. "Exorcizing the Family Demons" *The World and I*, (February 1993), 321–327.

Gray, Paul. "*Anil's Ghost*" (Book Review). *Time* 155.18 (May 1 2000), 75.

Heble, Ajay. 'Putting Together Another Family: *In the Skin of A Lion* and the Writing of Canadian (Hi)stories. *Esssays in Canadian Writing 56*, (Fall 1995), 236–254.

———. " 'Rumours of Topography': The Cultural Politics of Michael Ondaatje's *Running in the Family.*" *Essays on Canadian Writing*, (Michael Ondaatje Issue) 53 (Summer 1994), 186–203.

Herodotus. *The Histories*. Written approximately 450 B.C. ed. A de Selincourt. Harmondsworth: Penguin, 1972.

Hutcheon, Linda. *Interview with Michael Ondaatje*. L. Hutcheon ed., *In Other Solitudes*. Toronto, Oxford, New York: Oxford University Press, 1990:179–203.

Jacobs, J. U. "Exploring, Mapping and Naming in Postcolonial Fiction: Michael Ondaatje's *The English Patient.*" *Nomina Africana*, 8.2 (1994) 1–7.

Jewinski, Ed. *Michael Ondaatje: Express Yourself Beautifully, A biography*. Toronto: ECW Press, 1994.

Kanaganayakam, Chelva. "A Trick With a Glass: Michael Ondaatje's South Asian Connection." *Canadian Literature*, 132 (Spring 1992), 33–42.

Kipling, Rudyard. *Kim*. First printed 1901, edition used. London: Macmillan, 1966.

Maver, I. "Creating the National in the International Context: the Postmodernity of Michael Ondaatje's Fiction." *Commonwealth Essays and Studies*, 17.2 (1995). 58–66.

Overbye, Karen. "Re-Membering the Body: Constructing the Self as Hero in *In the Skin of A Lion.*" *Sudies in Canadian Literature*, 17.2 (1992/3), 3–13.

Scobie, Stephen. "Two Authors in Search of A Character: bp Nichol and Michael Ondaatje"[on treatment of Billy the Kid]. Solecki, Sam ed. *Spider Blues: Essays on Michael Ondaatje*. Montreal: Vehicule Press, 1985.

Solecki, Sam. *Spider Blues: Essays on Michael Ondaatje*. Montreal: Vehicule Press, 1985.

Spearey, Susan. "Mapping and Masking: The Migrant Experience in Michael Ondaatje's *In the Skin of A Lion.*" *Journal of Commonwealth Literature*, 29.2 (1994)

Sugunasiri, Suwanda, H. J. "Sri Lankan Poets: 'The Bourgeoisie that Fled the Revolution.'" *Canadian Literature*. 132 (Spring 1992), 61–79.

Tait, Theo. *"Anil's Ghost"* (Book Review). *The London Review of Books*, 22.14 (July 20 2000), 39–40.

Updike, John. *"Anil's Ghost"* (Book Review). *The New Yorker*, 76.11 (May 15 2000), 91–2.

Wachtel, Eleanor. "An Interview with Michael Ondaatje." *Essays on Canadian Writing*, (Michael Ondaatje Issue) 53 (Summer 1994), 250–261.

York, Lorraine M. "Whirling Blindfold in the House of Woman: Gender Politics in the Poetry and Fiction of Michael Ondaatje."*Essays on Canadian Writing*, (Michael Ondaatje Issue) 53 (Summer 1994), 71–91.